Lemonade Launch: Bobby's Business Breakthrough

By Cinncinnius

Sour Start

Bobby Lemons was brimming with the sort of infectious enthusiasm that only a ten-year-old with a summer vacation plan could muster. He had seen it in movies and read it in books: the quintessential lemonade stand, a staple of entrepreneurial spirit and youthful ambition. With the mercury climbing and his desire to afford the latest video game, he saw no better way to both beat the heat and earn some pocket money than setting up his very own stand.

His parents had humored his business proposal, providing him with a small table, a brightly colored umbrella to shield him from the unforgiving sun, and enough lemons, sugar, and paper cups to start off his small venture. In Bobby's eyes, there was no possibility of failure; he was as eager to quench the neighborhood's thirst as he was to fill his piggy bank.

He spent hours juicing lemons by hand, carefully measuring out sugar, and chilling pitchers of his homemade concoction to perfection. The stand was stationed at the end of his driveway, adorned with a hand-painted sign that read 'Bobby's Lemonade - Only 50¢!'. From his standpoint, anyone zooming by or strolling in the blistering heat would surely be tempted by the promise of an ice-cold refreshment.

But as the day wore on, reality began to take a sip out of Bobby's optimism. The morning rush he had anticipated never materialized. Neighbors ambled by, offering polite smiles and nods, but few stopped to indulge in his lemony brew. The noonday sun bore down mercilessly, warming the pitchers despite the shade from his umbrella. With each passing hour, the ice cubes in his cooler melted a little more, much like his hopes.

Bobby had managed to sell a couple of cups to the Johnson twins from next door, who were just looking for a way to escape their mother's summer-cleaning wrath. But two sales were not enough to call his venture a success. Disheartened, he stirred his lemonade listlessly, sending ice cubes clinking against the sides of the pitcher—a melancholy melody to accompany his burgeoning realization that perhaps the lemonade business wasn't as sweet as he thought.On the summer-kissed sidewalks of Maple Street, Bobby Lemons' stand—a vibrant splash of yellow and green—stood optimistically between towering oaks. A handmade sign, with letters dancing in a clumsy harmony, beckoned 'Fresh Lemonade - Only 50 cents!' Yet, beneath the playfulness of crayon and marker, a business challenge was unraveling. Bobby's determination seemed as untouched as many of the plastic cups he'd painstakingly stacked that morning. He'd envisioned a different scene: lines of thirsty neighbors, coins clinking into his money jar, and endless rounds of pouring and serving. Instead, Bobby was learning his first lesson in business: reality could be a stubborn customer.

With his baseball cap pulled low against the glare of the afternoon sun, Bobby watched cars pass by with only the occasional slowing— a pause of consideration before they sped off again, leaving behind only the scent of exhaust and heat shimmers on the asphalt. He checked his watch, a birthday gift that suddenly felt heavy on his wrist. It was nearing three in the afternoon, and Bobby calculated his net earnings—just enough for half a comic book. His heart sank; at this rate, he'd need to save all summer for the new bike he'd been dreaming of.

Every so often, a pedestrian would meander close, a neighbor out for a stroll or a jogger taking a break, but after a brief exchange of pleasantries or a cursory glance at the sign, they'd press on. Bobby couldn't fathom it—his lemonade was sweet, tangy, with just the right kick to refresh the soul on a sizzling day. Still, his pride and confusion were secondary to the crumpled dollar bills and sparse change in his cash box.

'Why won't they stop?' he wondered aloud, the frustration clear in his voice as he addressed no one in particular. He considered the possibility that perhaps his location was not ideal, or the price too steep for an impulse buy. Maybe, Bobby thought with a slump in his shoulders, running a business required more than enthusiasm and a good recipe.

Then, as if the day were a stage and Bobby's struggle the main plot, a familiar figure appeared around the bend. Mr. Vozar, Bobby's teacher, often took these long ambles through the neighborhood after school. A keen observer with spectacles perched on the bridge of his nose, he noticed the wilted look on Bobby's face from a distance. With a gentle smile and a gait that seemed in no hurry, he approached the lemonade stand, curious to see how his pupil was managing in the throes of entrepreneurship. With a warm nod, Mr. Vozar rested his hands on the homemade counter of the stand. 'Your first venture into the world of commerce, Bobby?' he asked with a twinkle in his eye. Bobby sighed, nodding his head slowly as he recounted his lackluster sales. 'Seems like I might have to shut down before I even start, Mr. Vozar.' He gestured towards the pitcher of lemonade, which remained three-quarters full despite the scorching sun.

Mr. Vozar uncapped the bottle of water he had in hand, taking a small sip before replying. 'Well, let's start with the basics. How much are you selling your lemonade for?' Bobby perked up a little at the question. '50 cents a cup - it's good lemonade, made with real lemons.' Mr. Vozar nodded approvingly but then looked around, as if to appraise the location. 'And how have you advertised your stand?' Bobby's face fell slightly. 'I made a sign and put it up here.' He pointed to the cardboard advertisement that leaned, slightly bent, against the front of the table.

'Hmm, I see,' Mr. Vozar muttered, rubbing his chin thoughtfully. 'Well, there's your first lesson, Bobby. Visibility and marketing are crucial in attracting customers. That sign needs to be where people can see it as they approach, not just when they are already in front of your stand.' Bobby listened intently, the cogs in his mind already turning with new ideas.

He looked at his hand-painted sign. The colors were cheerful, and his handwriting was neat, but it was true that unless someone was already at the stand, they may not notice it from the street. 'What else can I do, Mr. Vozar?' he asked eagerly.

Mr. Vozar chuckled softly, his eyes scanning the quiet street. 'Well, you've got to think about your target audience. Who's most likely to want a refreshing drink on a hot day like today?' The teacher paused, giving Bobby a chance to think. 'Kids playing outside, people working in their yards, joggers?' Bobby offered.

'Exactly!' Mr. Vozar exclaimed. 'Now, how can you reach them? Think bigger than just a sign. There are fliers, word of mouth, special offers...lots of ways to let people know about your product.' Bobby's spirits lifted as he realized that this wasn't the end of his lemonade stand; it was just the beginning.

The rest of the afternoon was a lesson in itself. Mr. Vozar stayed with Bobby, sharing tips and encouraging him to interact with the occasional passerby, not just with the hope of making a sale but to engage with potential customers, learning about their likes and dislikes. Although the day ended with only a few more cups sold, Bobby felt a flicker of hope. He had knowledge now, something to build on. Tomorrow would be a new day, and with Mr. Vozar's guidance, it could be the start of something great.Bobby listened with rapt attention as Mr. Vozar painted a picture of what a successful business could look like. 'Visibility, Bobby, is crucial,' Mr. Vozar explained, gesturing emphatically. 'Your sign needs to stand out, capture attention. Think about the placement. Think about colors that pop and words that resonate.' Bobby nodded, his brain buzzing with ideas. 'And what about your recipe? Have you asked customers what they think?' Mr. Vozar continued. 'Maybe they prefer it sweeter, or perhaps they're looking for a low-sugar option. Understanding your customers' preferences can set you apart.'

Bobby thought about the lemonades he'd tasted at the county fair. There were so many different kinds! Maybe he could experiment with flavors or even offer a 'lemonade of the day' special. He shared the idea with Mr. Vozar, who smiled approvingly. 'Great thinking! That's adding value to your product, which can justify a better price or bring in more curious customers. Remember, your customers are your best form of marketing. If they love what you're doing, they'll tell others.' The idea of word-of-mouth marketing ignited another spark in Bobby.

As they continued brainstorming, Mr. Vozar delved into the concept of operating costs. 'You need to factor in the cost of lemons, sugar, water, even those cups you're using,' he said, tapping a stack of plastic cups. 'How much does each cup of lemonade cost you to make?' This made Bobby furrow his brow; he hadn't thought about it like that before. They calculated it together, and Bobby was surprised to find out that his costs were higher than he realized. 'Understanding your costs is how you set the right price,' Mr. Vozar explained. 'You need to make sure you're not just recovering what you spend, but also making a profit to reinvest back into your stand.'

The day was drawing to a close, colors melting into a dusky hue. Bobby thanked Mr. Vozar for his invaluable advice. 'We'll start first thing tomorrow. Implement these changes and I bet you'll see a difference,' Mr. Vozar said with a confident nod. 'Remember, Bobby, every successful person started with a dream and a whole lot of learning. You're on the right path.' With that, Mr. Vozar patted Bobby on the shoulder and walked off into the warm evening, leaving Bobby to ponder the vast sea of possibilities before him.

An Unlikely Mentor

The next morning arrived with a golden shine that seemed to promise prosperity and new beginnings. Bobby Lemons was awake before the sun had even made its full appearance above the horizon. Charged with the advice of Mr. Vozar, he was determined to apply the lessons he had learned to his little lemonade enterprise. With a fresh notepad in hand, he began jotting down the strategies they had discussed.

Firstly, he decided to improve the visibility of his lemonade stand. He took out his paintbrushes, some bright yellow and green paints, and got to work on a new, eye-catching sign that read, 'Bobby's Fresh Lemonade!' in bold, whimsical letters. Once it dried, he placed it strategically so that it could be seen from both ends of the street.

Next, Bobby considered the preferences of his customers. What did they enjoy the most? Classic lemonade was a hit, but perhaps they wanted variety? He resolved to experiment with new recipes—adding fresh mint, trying out a blend with iced tea, and even a touch of honey for those with a sweet tooth. He knew it was important to engage with his customers, to ask for their opinions, and even offer free samples of new concoctions to draw them in.

Marketing was next on his agenda. 'It's not just about selling lemonade, it's about telling a story,' Mr. Vozar had said. So, Bobby decided to create little flyers that narrated the steps of how he made his lemonade, with an emphasis on 'fresh', 'homemade', and 'from the heart.' He posted these flyers around the neighborhood, hoping to create a sense of community around his stand.

Lastly, the numbers. Bobby began to calculate his costs of goods (COGS), his expected revenue, and how to price his lemonade to ensure both satisfaction for customers and a profit for himself. He scrutinized the expenses down to the last cent, and the exercise revealed opportunities for savings he hadn't seen before. He could buy lemons in bulk, make his own ice, and even use his grandmother's garden herbs for the infused drinks.

By the time the street was humming with the sounds of the early risers, Bobby was ready. He stood by his revamped stand, a blend of youthful hope and newfound savvy, waiting for his first customer of the day.

It didn't take long for people to notice the changes. 'Wow, look at your stand, Bobby!' Mrs. Agnes, the neighbor who always took her dog for a walk in the morning, exclaimed as she approached. 'This new sign is delightful! And what's this about mint lemonade?' She was intrigued, and that's exactly the response Bobby was hoping for.Mrs. Agnes, in her lavender scented dress and her poodle, Duchess, in tow, couldn't resist the charm of the new lemonade stand. 'Well, I must say, I've never heard of mint lemonade before - I'll have to give it a try!' With a smile that could light up any cloudy day, Bobby poured her a chilled cup of his latest concoction, the faint aroma of fresh mint mingling with the tang of lemons wafting up to greet her. She took a sip and immediately, her eyes brightened. 'Oh, my stars, Bobby, this is heavenly! You've got yourself something special here.'

Encouraged by the compliment, Bobby engaged her further. 'Thank you, Mrs. Agnes! I'm trying something new, you see. Do you think it's something that people would enjoy on a regular scale?' Mrs. Agnes paused, considering the question while Duchess took a polite interest in a nearby fire hydrant. 'I believe so, dear. It's refreshing and different - just the kind of thing people look for on a hot summer day.'

Their conversation was joined by Mr. Jenkins, the postman, who overheard the praise. 'What's this I hear about a special lemonade?' he asked, wiping sweat from his brow with a handkerchief. Bobby explained the idea behind his infused flavors, and handed Mr. Jenkins a cup of ginger-lemon fizz. The postman, usually a man of few words, was surprisingly verbose after his first sip. 'Zesty! Kid, you're onto something. It's got a kick that'll wake you up better than morning coffee.'

Between customers, Bobby kept busy replenishing his supplies, noting down their feedback, and adjusting the amounts for the next batch accordingly. Some preferred sweeter tastes, others looked for a stronger lemon kick, and a few adventurous souls were eager to sample whatever new twist Bobby managed to dream up. His notebook was fast becoming scribbled with notes on preferences, suggestions, and the ever-important sales numbers.

By midday, the sun had climbed to its zenith, and the flow of customers grew from a trickle to a steady stream. Word of mouth had begun to work its magic, and Bobby's lemonade became the talk of the neighborhood. Curiosity brought people, but the quality of his drinks made them stay, and soon there was a small queue forming at the stand. Bobby handled the crowd with aplomb, taking orders, serving drinks, and making change with a dexterity that belied his age.

It was during this busy swell that Mr. Vozar reappeared, leaning against a light pole, observing the young entrepreneur at work. Sporting a faint smile, he watched as Bobby conversed, sold, and even dealt with the occasional spill or shortage with a calmness that spoke volumes of the lessons he'd imparted. After a lull, he made his way forward. 'Bobby, how are you managing with the demand?'

Bobby looked up from his cash box, a mix of pride and fatigue in his eyes. 'Mr. Vozar! It's been amazing. I've had to make more lemonade three times already!' The teacher nodded approvingly. 'That's supply and demand for you. You're doing well, but remember to keep your inventory in check—you don't want to run out of product or have too much that it goes to waste.'

'I've been tracking everything right here,' Bobby said, tapping his notebook. 'And adjusting prices based on how well things are selling.' Mr. Vozar's smile grew wider at the young man's diligence.

'Excellent. The lessons are paying off, aren't they?'Mr. Vozar's question lingered in the air as an encouragement rather than a challenge, 'They certainly are!' Bobby replied enthusiastically. As the day wore on, Bobby felt a surge of energy each time he filled a glass with his tangy, sweet concoction. Sales continued to soar, but with the influx of customers came a new set of issues to navigate. Bobby, with Mr. Vozar's advice in mind, found himself constantly checking his stock of lemons, sugar, and ice.

With every sale, he made a small mark in his notebook, tallying his supplies against the demand. The lessons on supply and demand became much more tangible with each mark. He learned to predict when he'd need to prepare more lemonade, keeping just enough ahead of the curve to avoid long wait times for his customers. But maintaining this delicate balance was trickier than he'd expected. Sometimes, he miscalculated the lemons needed, or overestimated how much ice would last through the scorching afternoon. 'It's like a see-saw,' Bobby murmured to himself, 'trying to stay perfectly balanced.'

As Mr. Vozar observed, he offered insights. 'Think about patterns,' he suggested gently, 'Do you notice more people coming during certain times of the day?' Bobby thought about it and realized there were indeed rushes at specific moments – right after school and later in the evening when folks were returning from work. 'Maybe I can prepare larger batches just before those times,' he pondered aloud. 'Exactly,' Mr. Vozar encouraged, 'Anticipating your customers' needs will help you manage your inventory more efficiently.'

Just then, Mrs. Matilda, who organized the local community events, approached the stand. She tasted the lemonade and her eyes gleamed with delight. 'Bobby, dear, this is delightful! How would you like to provide lemonade at our next community gathering? It's a perfect occasion to showcase your business.' The opportunity was golden, and Bobby could hardly contain his excitement. He glanced at Mr. Vozar, seeking reassurance. 'It's a fantastic opportunity, Bobby,' he affirmed, 'It will surely increase your visibility.'

The remainder of the day was a blur as Bobby worked to perfect his product. He began to brainstorm ideas for the event, which could be a turning point in his entrepreneurial journey. He would need to figure out pricing for larger quantities, transportation of supplies, and, of course, how to manage the expected increase in demand. 'This is going to require some serious planning,' Bobby mused, feeling slightly overwhelmed but determined. 'But I'm ready for it.' As the sun dipped below the horizon, he closed his stand, tired but filled with a sense of accomplishment and excitement for the opportunities ahead. The next step of his journey was just beginning, and he was eager to take it on. The next morning, Bobby was up with the sun. His notebook was already teeming with lists and diagrams by the time Mr. Vozar strolled by. The older man's eyebrows rose in surprise. 'Well, well, Bobby! This looks like some battle plan!' he exclaimed, peering over the crowded pages.

Bobby grinned up at him. 'Morning, Mr. Vozar! Just trying to get a handle on everything for the big day!' Mr. Vozar nodded approvingly and took a seat on the stool next to the stand. 'Let's go over it, then. You've got an event to dazzle.'

Together, they went over Bobby's notes. He had broken down the costs of lemons, sugar, ice, and cups, trying to find the best price for his lemonade that would cover his costs and leave a profit. Mr. Vozar suggested he think of ways to streamline his process for the event to serve more people faster. 'Efficiency is key when you've got a queue,' Mr. Vozar pointed out, 'and you'll have one, I'm sure of it.'

They discussed the concept of 'economies of scale', with Bobby learning that buying in bulk could reduce his cost per lemonade. Mr. Vozar used a stick to draw a graph in the dirt to illustrate the concept, and Bobby's face lit with understanding.

Following Mr. Vozar's advice, Bobby arranged with Mrs. Matilda to visit the event location to get a lay of the land. They explored where his lemonade stand would be situated and how he'd accommodate the larger crowds. He imagined lines of people, all there to taste his lemonade.

The week before the event was a blur of preparation. Bobby tested different recipes to make larger batches without sacrificing taste. He arranged for the delivery of supplies to the event site and sourced a small handcart to transport everything from his booth to the serving area. He developed a simple, streamlined order and payment process to handle multiple customers at once.

Each night, Bobby would recount his day's progress to his parents, excitement tingeing his words. His folks were proud, offering to help where they could. His dad helped build a sturdy sign that read 'Bobby's Fresh Lemonade: Squeeze the Day!' which they would set up at the event.

As the event day loomed closer, Bobby grew anxious yet excited. He knew that he was as prepared as he could be. He had followed Mr. Vozar's advice, worked hard, and learned a great deal in a short time. His confidence, like his business acumen, was blooming.

Finally, the day before the event, they did a dry run. Mr. Vozar acted as a stream of customers, while Bobby mixed, poured, collected payment, and sent satisfied customers on their way with smiles and lemonade. As the sun settled in the sky, washing the stand in golden light, Mr. Vozar clapped a hand on Bobby's shoulder. 'You're ready, Bobby. Tomorrow's going to be fantastic.'

Bobby gazed at his stand, now more of a portable booth, with a sense of pride swelling within him. 'Yeah,' he said, 'I think it really is going to be.'

Understanding Costs

The energetic chatter of early morning filled the air as Bobby dragged his well-stocked lemonade stand to the bustling community park. The locals were trickling in, creating a tapestry of noise as they prepared for the day's activities. Bobby felt a harmonious blend of nervous excitement and determination—he was ready to apply everything Mr. Vozar had taught him.

Early in the day, Mr. Vozar stopped by, carrying a small notepad and a pen. 'Good morning, Bobby! Are you all set for the big day?' he asked. Bobby nodded, his face beaming with eagerness. 'But there's one more important lesson I want to go over with you before we get caught up in the hustle and bustle. It's about tracking your costs of goods sold—otherwise known as COGS.' Bobby looked intently as Mr. Vozar continued, 'It's the total cost of everything you've spent to make your lemonade—your lemons, sugar, cups—all of it. Understanding your COGS will help you price your lemonade properly and figure out your profits.'

Bobby pulled out a notebook of his own, ready to make sense of the numbers that would be critical to his business. He began to carefully jot down the cost of a dozen lemons, a bag of sugar, and the set of cups he had purchased in bulk. Mr. Vozar guided him through calculating the cost per glass, and how to keep track of his inventory. 'Keep this updated throughout the day,' Mr. Vozar advised. 'It'll be a fundamental part of understanding your business.'

As the event grew more crowded, people began to queue before Bobby's stand, drawn by the fresh scent of citrus and the vibrant sign that read 'Bobby's Fresh Lemonade.' Customers smiled as they exchanged coins for a refreshing glass, and Bobby meticulously noted each sale, mentally subtracting the cost of goods from his earnings. Hour by hour, his confidence grew, but so did his exhaustion. It was a delicate dance of hand-to-lemon-to-cup, but he was finding his rhythm.

Though the sun climbed high and the day wore on, Bobby's enthusiasm persisted. He recalled Mr. Vozar's words about efficiency and customer service and kept a steady smile, even as he watched his stock dwindle. Making a quick estimate, he realized he was close to covering his COGS and inching towards profit. Excitement tinged his next interactions; he was not just selling lemonade, he was running a budding enterprise.

As the final hour of the event approached, Bobby's once-abundant pile of lemons had significantly reduced, and the sugar was nearing its end. His tracking notebook was almost full, each line a testament to a job well done. Mr. Vozar returned, his face a picture of pride. 'How did we do, Bobby?' he asked. Bobby showed him the notebook, his hand hovering over the last tally. 'We've done more than just sell lemonade today, Mr. Vozar. We've learned the value of every slice of lemon and every spoonful of sugar.' The elder man smiled, 'Exactly, Bobby. That's the heart of a successful business.'Mr. Vozar's eyes gleamed as he scanned each entry in the notebook. 'You see, Bobby,' he said as they sat in the quiet lull between customers, 'the Cost of Goods Sold, or COGS as we call it, isn't just about knowing what you're spending. It's about understanding how those costs relate to each sale.' He tapped the notebook. 'For each cup of lemonade sold, you now know exactly how much of that is pure profit and how much is recovering your inputs.'

Bobby nodded, absorbing every word. 'So if I find a way to get lemons for less, I make more per cup?' he asked earnestly.

'Exactly!' Mr. Vozar exclaimed. 'And it's the same with sugar, and cups, and any other materials you use. Economies of scale might come into play when you buy in larger quantities, which can decrease your COGS and increase your profits.'

They continued this back-and-forth, with Bobby's mind racing as the sun climbed higher in the sky. Time passed, and the lemonade stand's popularity didn't wane. By mid-afternoon, Bobby noticed his reserves dwindling rapidly. He whispered to Mr. Vozar, 'What do I do when I run out of stuff?'

Mr. Vozar pondered for a moment. 'In business, Bobby, predicting demand is vital. Now you know you've got a product people love, it's time to consider how you'll replenish your stock without missing a beat. That means finding a vendor, negotiating prices, maybe even creating a backstock.'

The next few hours were a whirlwind of activity. Bobby dashed to nearby stores with Mr. Vozar, comparing prices, calculating costs, and purchasing additional lemons, sugar, and cups. Back at the stand, he adjusted his tallies to account for the new supplies, maintaining a clear record despite the rush.

Sometimes, Bobby's classmates would stop by, asking for free cups of lemonade, but Bobby stood firm, explaining why he had to charge even his friends. 'Every cup has a cost,' he would say, sharing a lesson from Mr. Vozar.

As the evening approached and the community event began to wind down, Bobby and Mr. Vozar counted what was left. Bobby's excitement grew as they estimated the day's profits. He had sold out twice and required urgent restocking each time. 'You've done well,' Mr. Vozar said. 'But this is just a peek into the world of business. Your education has just begun.'

Bobby felt a surge of pride and determination. What had started as a simple venture had opened his eyes to a future full of possibilities. The stand may close for the day, but his entrepreneurial spirit was just getting started.As the last rays of the sun dipped below the horizon, marking the end of the community event, Bobby and Mr. Vozar settled in for a final, crucial task of the day - counting the day's earnings. 'It's just not about how much lemonade you've sold,' Mr. Vozar began, folding up his chair and moving closer to the table. 'It's also about understanding how much you've earned after all the costs.' Bobby nodded, his brows furrowed in concentration.

On the table lay a small pile of coins and bills, the tangible fruits of Bobby's labor. Next to it, he placed receipts from the day's purchases: a chronicle of lemons, sugar, and cups. 'So, this is all the money we made today,' Bobby said, pointing to the cash. Mr. Vozar corrected gently, 'That's your revenue, Bobby. It's the total amount of money received from sales before any expenses are subtracted.' Bobby's eyes widened as he absorbed the information.

Working together, they started to categorize and record each expense. It was a meticulous process, but as they tallied up the totals, a clearer picture of Bobby's business performance emerged. 'Okay, now subtract your costs from your revenue. That's your gross profit,' Mr. Vozar instructed. Bobby did the math and excitedly declared the number. It was less than the revenue, but still a good sum. 'Wow, so that's what I really earn from selling each glass?' Bobby was beginning to grasp the financial underpinnings of a business.

'Well, almost,' Mr. Vozar added, 'there are still other expenses like marketing, your time, and maybe rent, if you decide to set up shop elsewhere.' With this new knowledge, Bobby started re-evaluating his operations. He realized that a successful business wasn't just about making sales, it was about being smart with money.

By the time they finished, the once intimidating numbers had become a simple equation that Bobby could understand and use to measure his success. Mr. Vozar explained that the final piece of the puzzle, the net profit, would be what's left after all expenses, not just the cost of goods sold. 'Think of it as the money you keep in your pocket at the end of the day,' he said with a smile. As the stand's lights were turned off and the last numbers crunched, Bobby looked up at Mr. Vozar with newfound respect and gratitude. 'Thank you, Mr. Vozar. I think I'm ready for whatever comes next.'As the sun dipped below the horizon, casting a golden hue over Bobby Lemons' lemonade stand, the list of expenditures lay neatly written on a yellow notepad. With each line, Bobby's eyes widened at the realization of where his money was going. Cups, lemons, sugar— items that seemed so inconsequential alone—added up to a significant amount when combined. Mr. Vozar, arms crossed with a satisfied nod, watched Bobby's mental gears turn. 'Now, Bobby,' he began in an educator's patient tone, 'you know what COGS is and why tracking them is crucial to understanding your business's health. But remember, this is only the beginning.'

Bobby looked up, pen in hand, ready for the next lesson. 'Okay, Mr. Vozar, what's next?' he asked, eager to delve deeper into the world of business. Mr. Vozar cleared his throat and pointed to the list. 'Next, we talk about managing these costs. Finding the best prices for your supplies, negotiating deals, perhaps even buying in bulk could save you money in the long run.' Bobby's brow furrowed; he hadn't realized there were such strategies to purchasing.

Over the next hour, Mr. Vozar explained the concept of economies of scale and the power of negotiation. Bobby listened intently, making notes on his pad—reducing COGS meant more money left over. His teacher also emphasized the importance of quality. 'You cannot compromise the taste of your lemonade; that's your brand's promise,' Mr. Vozar cautioned. Bobby nodded in agreement, recalling a few customers complimenting the unique tangy-sweet blend of his drink. He didn't want to lose that signature flavor.

Before leaving, Mr. Vozar turned to Bobby and asked, 'How much do you think your time is worth, Bobby?' This question stumped him. Bobby had never thought to value his time in monetary terms. 'We will put a pin in that,' Mr. Vozar said with an enigmatic smile. 'Next time, we'll talk about your revenue, gross profit, and the subtleties of net profit. We'll go beyond lemons and sugar to renting spaces and adding marketing.' With the hint of challenges ahead, Bobby felt a spark ignite within him.

The stand now quiet, Bobby spent the remainder of the evening re-evaluating his costs and brainstorming ways to reduce them without compromising quality. He was starting to see his little lemonade stand not just as a summer pastime, but as a potential enterprise. And with each calculation and adjustment, he took another step toward turning Mr. Vozar's lessons into action. Armed with a newfound understanding of COGS, Bobby Lemons felt equipped to tackle the inefficiencies in his business head-on. That weekend, he went to the local warehouse store with his savings clutched in his hands. As he walked through the towering aisles, he made his selections carefully, reflecting on Mr. Vozar's advice about quality and quantity. After comparing prices and calculating costs, Bobby chose a bulk purchase of lemons, a large bag of sugar, and a stack of sturdy cups designed for cold beverages.

By buying in bulk, he quickly realized, he could lower his COGS considerably. He learned to be astute, noting the different prices per unit and understanding how buying larger quantities could save him money in the long run. This might mean a larger upfront cost, but he would be making a higher profit on each cup of lemonade sold. As he loaded his supplies into the family's minivan, he felt like he was laying the foundations of his own little business empire.

Back at the stand, Bobby decided to implement another one of Mr. Vozar's lessons: tracking COGS meticulously. He made a ledger from an old notebook he had, dedicating a page to each ingredient. Whenever he made a purchase, he noted it down, including the price and the quantity. He then tracked how many cups of lemonade each batch of ingredients made, giving him a clear picture of what each cup was costing him to produce. It was a tedious process, but as the numbers started to form patterns, Bobby felt a sense of control that he had never experienced before.

It wasn't just about lemons and sugar anymore. Understanding his costs meant that he was learning to make more informed decisions, like whether to buy lemons from the local farmer's market when the warehouse store ran a special promotion, or when to invest in better quality sugar when customers began to comment on the improved taste of his lemonade. Each decision was made with his bottom line in mind, always striving for the perfect balance between cost and quality.

As the day waned and the sun settled into a dusky pink, Bobby counted his earnings. They were the most he had ever made in a single day. This triumph, however, was not just in the numbers. It was in the understanding that these small victories were just the prologue to a grander narrative in the world of business. With a moment of pride swelling in his chest, he closed his ledger and looked up at the horizon, envisioning his future not just as a lemonade stand owner, but as a shrewd business owner who had learned to value every cent and every second.

'I see you're closing up shop for the day,' Mr. Vozar said, walking up just as Bobby was packing away his supplies. 'Looks like you've had quite the successful day.'

Bobby beamed back. 'It's all thanks to the lessons. And tomorrow, we're planning to dive into revenue and profits, right?'

'Right,' Mr. Vozar smiled. 'You're on your way, Bobby. Just remember, a good business isn't just about what you make, it's also about what you manage to keep.' With those closing words, Mr. Vozar gave Bobby a reassuring pat on the shoulder and left him to his thoughts of tomorrow's lesson and the many days after that would shape his entrepreneurial journey.

Crunching the Numbers

The next morning, Bobby was up with the sun, eager to put the new lessons into play. He squared his shoulders and manned his lemonade stand with a heightened sense of purpose. As he set up, he couldn't help but hum a little tune, a melody of optimism and determination.

But success in business, Bobby was about to learn, went beyond a sunny disposition and hard work. He needed a firm grasp of the more intricate details, the financials that truly told the story of a business's health—revenue, gross profit, and net profit. As the first customer of the day approached, Bobby poured a cup of his finest lemonade, anticipation swirling in his gut like the ice in his pitcher.

The day progressed and with each cup sold, Bobby marked a tally in his notebook. Sales were good, the sun was scorching, and the lemonade was a refreshing reprieve for the parched pedestrians. By noon, he had sold more than he had the entire previous day. But when Mr. Vozar appeared that afternoon, he had a different set of numbers to discuss.

'Let's talk about your revenue,' Mr. Vozar began, pulling up a chair. He took the notebook from Bobby and flipped through the pages. 'This number here, the total amount of money you've collected from sales—that's your revenue.'

Bobby nodded, proud of the figure. 'It's a lot bigger than last week,' he remarked, unable to hide the pride in his voice.

'Yes, it's impressive,' Mr. Vozar agreed, 'but it's not the whole picture. Now, we deduct your costs,' he continued, pointing to the list of expenses. 'The lemons, sugar, cups, and any other costs associated with making your lemonade. The number we're left with after that, is your gross profit. That's what you've earned before any other expenses are taken into account.'

A furrow knitted itself between Bobby's brows. 'But isn't that my earnings?' he asked, confusion mixing with curiosity.

'Partly,' Mr. Vozar explained. 'Your gross profit is important, but it doesn't consider additional expenses like marketing or wages if you decide to hire help. Once you deduct those, you have your net profit—the amount you truly keep as earnings.'

Bobby's pen danced across the page, subtracting numbers, his mind beginning to understand the difference between making sales and making a profit. The sense of understanding was crystallizing; the tallies of sales were just a starting point, not the finish line.

As the sun began to dip, and the hustle of customers slowed, Bobby leaned back against his chair, awed by the depth of knowledge he'd just plunged into. He realized now that a good day of sales didn't necessarily mean a good day for business—not if costs ate too much into the revenue.

That evening, with Mr. Vozar's help, Bobby crafted his first true financial statement. The numbers told a story different from the one he had imagined that morning, but it was a clearer, more accurate story of his lemonade stand's financial health.

'Tomorrow we'll discuss how to use these numbers to make better business decisions,' Mr. Vozar said as he packed up his briefcase. 'And we'll touch on marketing—how to attract even more customers to your most excellent lemonade.'

As the light faded, so did Bobby's doubts. With every lesson, he was becoming not just a lemonade stand owner but a fledgling entrepreneur.Bobby spent the night tossing and turning, his dreams a kaleidoscope of numbers: revenues, costs, profits. What had once been the simple act of selling lemonade had unfolded into something far more complex, and intriguing. With the sun painting a golden hue across his bedroom wall, Bobby was awake before his alarm had a chance to sound. His mind was buzzing: today, he would learn about making informed business decisions and begin to dabble in the world of marketing.

Mr. Vozar arrived promptly as usual, the afternoon heat already beginning to swell. 'Bobby,' he began, 'yesterday you learned about the importance of understanding your financials. Today, we go one step further. It's not enough to know what your profits are; you need to understand what those numbers can tell you about your business operations.' Bobby listened intently as his mentor explained the concept of analyzing expenses to find areas where he could reduce costs without compromising the quality of his lemonade.

'For instance,' Mr. Vozar said, pointing to a figure on the statement, 'your sugar cost is quite high. Have you thought about buying in bulk or finding a cheaper supplier?' Bobby's eyes widened with realization. He had been purchasing sugar from the corner store down the street, never questioning if he could get a better deal elsewhere.

After a thoughtful discussion about expenses, Mr. Vozar switched gears to focus on the gross and net profits. 'Your gross profit margins are good, Bobby. However, after all your expenses, your net profit is what you actually take home. Let's see if we can improve that by streamlining your operations and cutting unnecessary costs.' They brainstormed ideas, with Bobby scribbling notes fervently.

As the lesson wrapped up, it was clear that Bobby had a newfound appreciation for the intricacies of business finances. 'Now, let's consider your customers. Who is buying your lemonade now, and who else might be interested?' Mr. Vozar transitioned smoothly into the basics of marketing. 'You need to think about who your product appeals to and how you can reach them.' Bobby's head was full of ideas – from creating eye-catching signs to offering loyalty discounts.

By the end of the day, Bobby had a list of action items: research sugar suppliers, design new signs, and brainstorm a potential loyalty program. His lemonade stand was on the precipice of transformation, and Bobby couldn't wait to get started.

As the sun dipped below the horizon, Bobby watched his small stand with pride. His thoughts were interrupted by a neighbor walking by. 'I saw you working with Mr. Vozar. He's a smart man. He must be teaching you a lot,' she said with a smile. Bobby grinned back, filled with a sense of purpose. 'Yes, he is. Tomorrow I'm going to start changing things around here. I want everyone to love my lemonade.' His eyes gleamed with the determination of a young entrepreneur on the cusp of success. That very evening, after the neighbor had strolled away, Bobby sat down at his kitchen table and began researching. He browsed through several online forums and local business listings, searching for a sugar supplier with lower prices that could reduce his cost of goods sold. He knew that if he could get his ingredients for less, he could either lower his prices to attract more cost-conscious customers or maintain current prices to increase his profit margin. After hours of comparisons and contemplation, Bobby found a wholesaler in the neighboring town that promised high-quality sugar at a rate nearly 15% cheaper than his current supply. He made a note to visit them early in the morning.

The next day, armed with a wad of saved-up allowance, Bobby pedaled his bike to the wholesaler. The warehouse was enormous, surrounded by crates of goods being loaded and unloaded. Bobby walked up to the sales counter, taking a deep breath before conversing with the representative. His confidence quivered slightly, but he recollected Mr. Vozar's advice on negotiation. After some back and forth, Bobby managed to secure an even lower rate by offering to promote the wholesaler's brand at his stand. He cycled back home, victorious, his backpack bulging with packets of bargain-priced sugar.

Emboldened by his success, Bobby decided that his next task was to revamp his marketing materials. He sketched a cheerful lemon on a blank piece of paper, alongside a bold tagline: 'Bobby's Lemonade: Squeeze the Day!' He used bright colors to make the flyers stand out and included a special offer for the first 10 customers of the day. He spent the rest of the afternoon distributing the flyers around the neighborhood, pinning them to community boards, and handing them out at the local park. His efforts were greeted with smiles and words of encouragement, further fueling his determination.

In the evening, Bobby sat down with a list of his regular customers, contemplating Mr. Vozar's suggestion of a loyalty program. He designed simple punch cards - 'Buy 9 cups get the 10th free!' - and prepared a small sign to advertise the program. He was thrilled at the thought of seeing his customers' faces light up when he handed them their loyalty cards the next day.

As night fell, Bobby's mind raced with possibilities. His lemonade stand was no longer just a summer pastime but a real business. And as he drifted off to sleep, visions of lemonade stands on every corner and a brand name synonymous with quality and fun danced in his dreams.The morning air was crisp as Bobby set up his lemonade stand, the anticipation of the day making his hands tremble slightly. He meticulously arranged his new marketing materials—a colorful banner with his brand name 'Bobby Lemons' splayed in a cheerful font, and neatly stacked flyers to hand out to passersby. Bobby also had his new punch cards at the ready, excited to offer them to his first customer of the day.

Bobby's first hour was slow, but he didn't allow discouragement to creep in. Instead, he smiled and handed out flyers to anyone who would take them. Then, just as he began to wonder if his efforts would pay off, a young mother with her two children approached. 'I saw your sign about the loyalty program,' she said, her interest piqued as she accepted a punch card. Her kids clamored for lemonade, and as they took their first sips, their faces broke into broad grins. 'Delicious!' the mother exclaimed, and Bobby's heart swelled with pride.

As more customers trickled in, Bobby began to track his sales and punch card distributions with more vigor. He took note of each transaction, mindful of Mr. Vozar's teachings about revenue and profit. He reminded himself that generating revenue was a start, but net profit was the finish line he was striving to cross.

By midday, Bobby had served several repeat customers, and the punch cards were a hit. He realized then that the loyalty program was not just a tactic to bring customers back, but also a way to build a relationship with them. His small stand was becoming a community fixture, and the sight of his regulars' smiles was as rewarding as the cash accumulating in his money box.

Late in the afternoon, as the sun began to dip lower in the sky, Bobby took a moment to tally his sales. He subtracted the cost of the new sugar and the printing expenses for his marketing materials from his revenue. What remained was his gross profit, but then he further subtracted his other expenses—lemons, cups, and stirrers—to find his net profit. The numbers made him giddy. Today, he had not only made sales, but he had also made a real profit.

As he packed up for the day, he felt a profound sense of accomplishment. Bobby Lemons and his lemonade stand were on a path to success. His teacher's lessons had taken root, and Bobby knew that every cup sold was a step towards his dream. He now understood the intricate balance between attracting customers and managing his finances. Tomorrow would be another day, and Bobby was already brewing ideas to continue his growth.The next morning, Bobby rose with the sun, a notebook in tow as he sat at his lemonade stand. He was eager to apply his newfound knowledge of revenue, gross profit, and net profit, and to investigate his customers' preferences. With every glass sold, he made a tick on his notepad, alongside notes on what they seemed to enjoy or request. Some loved the classic recipe, while others asked for a dash of mint or a squeeze of lime. Each insight was a clue in optimizing his lemonade offerings.

Throughout the day, Bobby saw a variety of customers, from joggers looking for a quick refreshment to parents buying a cup for their kids as an after-school treat. He engaged with them, asking for feedback, and paying attention to their habits. Despite the buzz of activity, he diligently recorded the sales, trying not to get distracted by the steady stream of coins clinking into his cashbox.

As the afternoon rolled into evening, Mr. Vozar swung by the stand, impressed by the business's activity. 'Bobby, it's bustling here!' he lauded, peering at the notes scattered around the counter. Taking the opportunity, Bobby shared his observations and sales records. Mr. Vozar nodded, 'Let's analyze this and see if there are patterns that can help you understand your customers even better.' They poured over the data together, discerning peak times and popular choices.

With Mr. Vozar's help, Bobby began to grasp the concepts of demand and customer satisfaction. It was one thing to sell lemonade; it was another to sell an experience that would bring people back. They discussed potential adjustments—perhaps offering 'flavor of the day' specials or a customer loyalty punch card. Bobby was ready to implement these ideas, his mind buzzing with the endless possibilities.

As the chapter ended, Bobby felt a new wave of enthusiasm. He was not just running a stand; he was cultivating a brand. The leap from making sales to sustaining a profitable business had begun, and Bobby Lemons was at the helm of his ship, navigating the entrepreneurial seas with newfound savvy.Bobby posted the 'Flavor of the Day' sign with pride. Raspberry Rush today, he decided. At first, customers were hesitant, but as the familiar tang of lemonade blended with the bursting notes of raspberry spread through their taste buds, their eyes lit up. Word of mouth traveled fast, and soon a steady line formed at the stand.

Mr. Vozar, who had observed the unfolding event, motioned Bobby over. 'See, you're creating a demand. But remember, with these specials, it's crucial to calculate your costs accordingly. Unique ingredients may cost more, and that affects your profits.' Bobby nodded, scribbling notes. He increased the price slightly for the special flavor, ensuring that his costs were covered and his profit margins remained healthy.

As the day progressed, Bobby introduced the loyalty punch card, which received an enthusiastic reception. After a customer's fifth purchase, they'd be entitled to a free lemonade. This not only encouraged repeat business but also gave Bobby a way to measure customer retention rates. Mr. Vozar was pleased. 'In business, repeat customers can be more valuable than one-time buyers. They become brand ambassadors.'

The sun began to dip below the horizon, and Bobby counted his day's takings. Revenue was certainly higher, but it was the calculation of net profit that had him grinning from ear to ear. After subtracting his expenses from the gross profit, the figure was undoubtedly favorable.

'Today was a good day,' Bobby said to Mr. Vozar, who replied with a knowing smile, 'It's not just about making money; it's about learning to sustain it. You're on the right path, Bobby. Keep this up.'

Bobby felt an immense sense of accomplishment. He was evolving from a mere seller to a shrewd businessman. He started dreaming of the future, of franchising, where stands just like his adorned street corners and parks, a buzzing yellow empire of lemony sweetness under the summer sun.

Expenses and Pricing

The next morning, a refreshed Bobby reopened his lemonade stand with the meticulousness of a seasoned entrepreneur. He arranged the cups in neat rows, ensured the ice was sufficiently stocked, and meticulously mixed the 'Flavor of the Day'—a tangy raspberry twist. But before the clamor of his first customers filled the air, Bobby took a moment to review his notes from the previous day.

Mr. Vozar, always timely, joined him, calculator and notepad in hand. 'Time to dig into the nitty-gritty of running a business, Bobby. Let's look at your expenses in detail and figure out the sweet spot for your pricing,' he said, a subtle excitement in his voice. Together, they listed down the costs: lemons, sugar, water, cups, and even the small amount he paid his friends who helped during peak times.

'You see, Bobby,' Mr. Vozar began, 'underpricing can be as harmful as overpricing. It's all about value perception and profit margin. Let's do some math and see where your current pricing lands us in terms of covering costs and making a profit.'

They broke down the cost of goods sold (COGS)—the direct costs attributable to the production of the lemonade. Bobby had never considered how each lemon or cup added to his expenses. When they compared the COGS to his current pricing, they found he was barely covering his costs, let alone making a substantial profit.

Mr. Vozar pointed out, 'Your lemonade is high quality—those organic lemons and pure cane sugar aren't cheap—so your price should reflect that. However, you can't price yourself out of the market either.' Bobby nodded, absorbing every word. 'So we need to find the price that covers your costs, pays you for your time and effort, and attracts customers—your ideal price point.'

Together, they explored competitive pricing. They looked at other lemonade stands in the area, at cafes selling similar drinks, and even at retail prices for bottled lemonade in stores. Through their research, Bobby realized his lemonade had a unique selling proposition—it was homemade, fresh, and used high-quality ingredients. They determined that a slight increase in his selling price would be justified, but he would need to communicate the value to his customers effectively.

As the sun crested over the canopy of trees that lined the park, Bobby displayed a new sign that read, 'Organic Lemonade Made Fresh Daily: Quality You Can Taste!' The slight pricing increase was now confidently displayed. He felt a twinge of nervousness but remembered Mr. Vozar's lesson about perceived value.

His first customer of the day eyed the new sign skeptically but upon sipping the lemonade, a look of sheer satisfaction spread across her face. 'Worth every penny!' she exclaimed, and Bobby's heart swelled. Word of mouth was quick and by the afternoon, his stand was busier than ever.

With the sun setting and the day's sales tallied, Bobby felt both exhausted and exhilarated. He counted his earnings, paid his friends, and put aside money for more supplies. The day's net profit had grown from the day before, and Bobby realized the pricing change had customers valuing his product even more.The satisfaction on the customer's face was more than just a confirmation for Bobby—it was a testament to his hard work and newly gained knowledge. Mr. Vozar stood beside the stand, arms crossed, observing the customers as they lined up and waited patiently for their glasses of lemonade. 'You see, Bobby,' began Mr. Vozar in a grown-up but gentle voice, 'determining the right price is a delicate balance. You've done well by considering the quality of your product and your competition.' Bobby nodded, feeling a mix of pride and relief. 'Yes, Mr. Vozar. It seems people don't mind paying a little extra for something they believe is worth it.'

As the afternoon waned, the stream of customers began to slow, allowing Bobby a moment to catch his breath. He took the opportunity to discuss with Mr. Vozar his plans for the future of the stand. 'I've been thinking about offering different flavors,' Bobby said hesitantly. 'Maybe selling cookies or other treats, too.' Mr. Vozar smiled, pleased to see Bobby thinking entrepreneurially. 'Those are great ideas, but remember, with new offerings come new costs, and potential changes to your COGS. Let's analyze today's sales data and use that to inform any new decisions.'

After the stand closed for the day, Bobby and Mr. Vozar studied the numbers. Bobby's business had doubled in revenue compared to the days before the pricing adjustment. Expenses had gone up slightly with the improved signage and higher-quality ingredients, but net profits still showed a remarkable increase. The higher price point had indeed made the lemonade seem more valuable, and customers were speaking loud and clear with their wallets. 'Looks like we have our own little case study here, Bobby. A prime example of how perceived value can impact sales,' remarked Mr. Vozar, initiating a mini business lesson right there on the sidewalk.

That evening, Bobby scrawled out ideas in his notebook, aiming to improve and expand his lemonade stand. Flavors like raspberry and peach danced in his head, but he knew getting too ahead of himself could be costly. He decided to approach one change at a time, starting with a survey to gauge customer interest in new flavors.

The next day, Bobby set out a small box with paper and a pen beside his lemonade stand with a sign reading, 'What flavors would you love to see at Bobby's Lemonade?'. The feedback was instantaneous and often enthusiastic, with many kids and adults alike dropping their flavor votes and suggestions into the box.

As he reviewed the flavor suggestions that evening, Bobby felt an entrepreneurial fire igniting within him. His little stand was evolving into something bigger, something potentially scalable. With Mr. Vozar's guidance, Bobby was learning that successful business wasn't just about having a good product but also about understanding the needs and desires of his customers. And at this moment, Bobby knew his lemonade stand was well on its way to becoming something extraordinary. The next day, Bobby couldn't wait to set out his lemonade stand. Mr. Vozar had given him homework: to monitor his expenses closely and to start testing a new price point. Armed with his ledger, calculator, and a new sense of determination, Bobby arrived early, ready to put his fresh knowledge to the test.

Before the first customer arrived, Mr. Vozar swung by with a smile. 'Ready for the day, Bobby?' He asked cheerfully. Bobby nodded, his eyes glancing toward the suggestion box, now bursting with paper slips scribbled with potential new flavors. 'It's going to be an exciting day.'

Mr. Vozar pulled up a chair and took out his notepad. 'Let's talk about expenses and pricing. Remember, you're running a business, and every penny counts. So, what are your expenses so far?' Bobby listed them out: lemons, sugar, ice, cups, and occasional maintenance for his stand. 'Good, good,' Mr. Vozar said, nodding as he jotted down notes. 'Now, let's discuss the pricing. What are you thinking?'

Bobby hesitated, 'Well, I was charging 50 cents per cup. But considering the costs and what I've observed of how much the other kids sell their drinks for, I think I should charge 75 cents.' Mr. Vozar raised his eyebrows, 'That's a decent jump. But let's think about the value you're offering. Your lemonade is freshly squeezed, and you're considering adding new flavors. That's worth something.'

They decided to try the new price point for the day. As customers trickled in, Bobby's nervousness transformed into confidence. Surprisingly, nobody batted an eye at the increased price. In fact, one customer even commented, 'Wow, this lemonade is great! Definitely worth the extra quarters.' By midday, Bobby realized that his revenue had increased significantly, without deterring his loyal customers.

Mr. Vozar used the momentum to discuss another critical concept: perceived value. 'Bobby, the price you set can also influence how customers perceive the quality of your lemonade. When they see that you take your product seriously and price it accordingly, they're more likely to believe it's of high quality. And rightfully so, because it is!' Bobby smiled, his mind racing with ideas on how to further enhance that perception.

By the day's end, Bobby had carefully recorded his expenses and revenues, finding that not only had his gross profit increased, but that he had also learned an invaluable lesson. The importance of calculating expenses accurately and the impact of pricing on his lemonade became clear to him as the sun dipped below the horizon. Tomorrow would be another day, another step in Bobby's journey — one where he would begin poring over the flavor suggestions and planning his marketing strategies with Mr. Vozar. For now, though, he relished the feeling of accomplishment looking at the day's tally, the boxes ticked, and the prospects that lay ahead. As the final customer of the day walked away with a cup of his best-selling lemonade, Bobby caught himself dreaming, not just of what his stand would become, but of the places it could take him.Early the next morning, Bobby was up with the sun, armed with a notepad full of customer suggestions and a newfound enthusiasm for business. Mr. Vozar arrived just as Bobby was setting up for the day, a stack of library books under his arm, all of them on marketing and small business success. They sat at the newly added picnic table beside the lemonade stand, already feeling like seasoned partners in business.

Together, they sifted through the pile of flavor suggestions, cherry-picking the ones they felt could become crowd favorites. 'What about a strawberry-lemon twist?' Bobby proposed, his eyes sparkling with creativity. Mr. Vozar nodded thoughtfully. 'That's good, but remember, whatever flavor we add now sets a precedent. We need to think about cost, preparation time, and whether it appeals broadly or only to a niche.' Bobby's nod was sober and considerate, far beyond his years.

Mr. Vozar shifted the topic to pricing. 'Your expenses are the foundation, but your price speaks to value. It's not just about covering costs; it's about what your customers are willing to pay for the experience of your lemonade.' They analyzed the competition, considering not just other lemonade stands but also local cafes and stores selling similar products. 'Where do we stand in terms of quality and price? Are we positioning ourselves as a premium product or a budget-friendly option?' These questions had Bobby's mind whirring.

After a lengthy discussion, they settled on a competitive price that struck a balance between affordability and the allure of a premium product. It was slightly above local competitors, but Bobby was confident the unique flavors and charm of his stand would justify it.

With pricing sorted, they delved into the realm of marketing. Drawing tactics from the books Mr. Vozar brought, they brainstormed ideas. 'What about a loyalty card?' Bobby suggested. 'Buy nine cups, get the tenth free?' Mr. Vozar beamed at the initiative. 'Brilliant! It encourages repeat business and makes customers feel valued.' They also discussed social media promotion, colorful signs, and partnering with other local businesses for cross-promotion.

As the stand's opening hours approached, they had a concrete marketing plan and were ready to test the waters with the new strawberry-lemon twist. The sweet tangy aroma filled the air as Bobby prepared the first batch. He could hardly wait to see the reactions of his customers, not just to the new flavor, but to the whole improved lemonade experience. It was a fresh chapter for Bobby Lemons, one that tasted promisingly sweet.When the clock struck ten in the morning, the sun cast a warm light over the pavement where Bobby's lemonade stand stood proudly. Today was different; today, the stand wasn't just a child's summertime hobby— it was the launchpad of a nascent entrepreneur's dream. Bobby placed a chalkboard sign by the sidewalk, its colorful letters spelling out 'Grand Unveiling: Strawberry-Lemon Twist! Try Our Loyalty

Program!'. He felt the flutter of butterfly wings in his stomach but steadied his nerves with a deep breath and a dusting of confidence Mr. Vozar had instilled in him.

The first customer of the day, a regular since the stand's inauguration, was Mrs. Peterson, a kindly older woman with a penchant for lemonade and neighborhood gossip. She eyed the new signage with interest. 'What's all this, Bobby? A new flavor, you say?' Her voice was laced with a mix of surprise and delight. Bobby beamed and poured her a sample. 'It's our latest concoction, Mrs. Peterson! I hope you enjoy it. And with every purchase, you'll get a stamp on your loyalty card—ten stamps, and you'll get a free glass!' Mrs. Peterson's eyes twinkled as she took a sip, and the expression that followed was one of unadulterated pleasure. 'Oh, that is simply delightful, dear! I'll certainly be coming back for more.' She declared, taking an extra card for her husband.

Word of mouth spread quickly in the small neighborhood, and soon enough, a steady stream of people from all walks of life made their way to Bobby's stand. The loyalty cards were a hit, as was the engagement on social media where Mr. Vozar had taught Bobby to post engaging content and interact with his followers. The stand even caught the attention of a local bakery, which proposed a deal to provide fresh pastries to sell alongside the lemonade. Cross-promotion began to weave its way into the fabric of Bobby's burgeoning enterprise.

As the sun began to dip lower in the sky, Bobby took a moment to analyze his day. He had run out of strawberry-lemon twist twice, and needed to order more supplies to keep up with the demand. The loyalty cards were nearly half gone, and he had gained several new followers online. It wasn't just about the lemonade anymore—it was about building relationships and a brand that people trusted and enjoyed. Bobby knew that this was just the beginning, and as he tallied up his earnings and expenses for the day, a sense of pride swelled within him. He was no longer just Bobby Lemons, the kid with a lemonade stand; he was Bobby Lemons, the young entrepreneur with dreams as big as the sky.

As they closed up shop for the day, Mr. Vozar patted Bobby on the back. 'Well done, Bobby. You've taken the first big step towards a future that's yours to shape. Remember, it's not just about the sales, but also the smiles you bring to people's faces.' Bobby watched the sun's last rays disappear, feeling the glow of accomplishment and the thrilling possibility of what tomorrow would bring.

Marketing 101

The next morning found Bobby bustling about his lemonade stand, infused with a fresh zest for improving his business. His eyes were bright with the reflection of the newly placed posters around the neighborhood, each one flamboyant with a burst of yellow and a catchy tagline: 'Squeeze the Day with Bobby's Lemonade!' Bobby had stayed up late sketching out designs and slogans, and with Mr. Vozar's help, they had created eye-catching visuals that were now peppered throughout the community.

Mr. Vozar arrived with a box of fresh lemons and a twinkle in his eye. 'I see you've been busy, Bobby. Those posters look fantastic! Now, let's talk about another important aspect of business: marketing.' Bobby's mind was an eager sponge, ready to soak up every lesson. 'Marketing is all about connecting with your customers and creating a desire for your product. It's not enough to have the best lemonade; people need to know about it and want it,' explained Mr. Vozar.

Bobby listened intently as Mr. Vozar detailed the tactics of successful marketing campaigns. They discussed the importance of a unique selling proposition (USP) and how Bobby's strawberry-lemon twist was an excellent example. They explored different mediums, from flyers and posters to word-of-mouth and social media. 'Word-of-mouth is particularly powerful. It's the personal recommendation from someone you trust. For that, your lemonade doesn't just have to taste good; it has to create an experience worth talking about.'

Eager to see the theory in practice, Bobby focused on engaging with each customer, asking for feedback, and gently encouraging them to share their experience with friends and family. He noticed some customers returning, bringing new faces along. It was a living lesson in the power of word-of-mouth that filled Bobby with elation. 'They're not just buying lemonade; they're buying into an experience, an idea…' Bobby pondered out loud. 'Exactly,' Mr.

Vozar nodded, 'and that's what makes a business thrive.'Bobby had
started to understand the importance of marketing and how it was
much more than just telling people about his lemonade stand. Mr.
Vozar had instilled in him an appreciation for crafting a story around
his brand. 'Your lemonade stand is more than a spot on the sidewalk;
it's the epicenter of community refreshment,' Mr. Vozar had said
with a twinkle in his eye. He advised Bobby to think of his stand as a
beacon that would draw in the weary and the thirsty with the promise
of an oasis in the form of a cold, refreshing glass of lemonade.

One sunny afternoon, Bobby decided to implement his first
major marketing initiative. He designed and crafted a bright, colorful
sign that read, 'Bobby Lemons' Thirst-Quenching Lemonade – More
Than Just a Drink, It's a Citrus Sensation!' He placed the sign at the
corner of the street, guiding potential customers toward the stand
with playful arrows and enticing illustrations of juicy, glistening
lemons.

But the sign was just the beginning. Mr. Vozar had taught
Bobby about promotions and the allure of limited-time offers. Bobby
decided to create the 'Lemons for Grades' program where students
could get discounts based on their latest report card grades. An 'A'
would earn them a 20% discount, a 'B' a 10%, and so on. This
initiative was more than just a marketing strategy; it started
conversations in homes, at schools, and even between parents at the
local grocery store.

His next move took a bit of courage. Bobby stood at the
busiest intersection near his stand, handing out free samples of his
lemonade. 'Try a taste of summer!' he would call out, as smiling
passersby slowed down to accept his offerings. These interactions
often turned into longer conversations, and many samplers turned
into customers, heading over to the stand to purchase their own full-
sized glass.

All these efforts were revolutionary for Bobby's small
operation and the results were undeniable. Sales started to climb, and
Bobby found that even he was surprised by the steady influx of new

customers. However, it wasn't just the numbers that changed; the atmosphere at Bobby Lemons' stand transformed. It became a hub where people lingered to chat with Bobby and each other, sipping slowly on their lemonade, savoring not just the taste but the communal experience. 'They're not just buying lemonade; they're becoming a part of something special,' Bobby realized.

With Mr. Vozar's guidance, Bobby also set up a 'Lemon Loyalty' reward card. For every ten glasses purchased, the customer would get the eleventh free. He distributed these to all his buyers, and the response was overwhelmingly positive. Kids were especially intrigued, often pooling their purchases to reach the free lemonade faster.

Word-of-mouth had indeed begun to power his business, forging a path that could only lead upward. Bobby jotted down every interaction, lesson, and result in a notebook—a compilation of success tactics that he could refer to as his business grew.

As the chapter came to a close, Bobby stood behind his lemonade stand, beaming with pride as his once-struggling venture was now bustling with activity. He had learned an invaluable lesson from Mr. Vozar: marketing was about much more than selling a product; it was about creating a story that people wanted to be a part of. With the newfound success of Bobby's lemonade stand, the demand for his delicious concoctions outstripped what he'd ever imagined, especially for the beloved strawberry-lemon twist. From the corner of his eye, he could easily spot customers who returned more frequently, eager to redeem rewards from their 'Lemon Loyalty' cards. Bobby quickly realized that he needed to manage his increased supply needs, and yet, the thought of expanding brought a twinge of fear. How would he maintain the quality that his customers had come to expect?

Sensing his student's quiet apprehension, Mr. Vozar initiated a new lesson. 'Bobby, scaling a business is like growing a plant; you need the right balance of resources and care,' he began, his voice filled with encouragement. 'You've already shown great skill in adapting. Remember the principles you've learned, and apply them to this next challenge. You'll find ways to streamline your process without losing your personal touch.'

Bobby listened intently, absorbing every word, knowing that this was the essence of entrepreneurship—evolving with the needs of the business while staying true to its roots. The following week was brimming with activity and learning. Bobby hired his first employee, a neighborhood friend who shared his passion for lemonade. He negotiated with local farmers for bulk purchases of lemons and strawberries, ensuring a steady supply while keeping costs down.

He also adapted his production techniques, creating larger batches without sacrificing the taste he'd so carefully crafted. Customers noticed the efficiency but were pleased to find the lemonade as refreshing as ever. As days blended into weeks, Bobby's operation became a well-oiled machine, his brand synonymous with both quality and innovation.

One balmy Saturday, as he watched a line of customers eagerly chatting while waiting for their turn at the stand, Bobby realized he had crossed an important threshold. His venture wasn't just a stand—it was a community staple. He felt a surge of gratitude. For every smile and thank you he received, his commitment to his business deepened.

The afternoon sun dipped lower in the sky, casting a golden hue over the stand. The buzz of conversation ebbed into a contented murmur as the day started to wind down. Bobby took this moment of calm to reflect on the journey so far. His notebook was thicker now, filled with scribbles of innovations, tweaks, and customer feedback. Through all the changes, it was the loyal support of his community and the wise guidance of Mr. Vozar that steadied his course.

He turned the page, ready to jot down the latest insight when a little girl, pink ribbon in her hair, approached him shyly. 'Excuse me, are you Bobby Lemons?' He looked down and smiled, 'That's me!' Her grin spread wide, 'I just wanted to say, your lemonade made me love lemons! Can I have another glass?' Such simple words, yet they carried the weight of success. Bobby served her a glass, knowing that each happy customer was another chapter in his ever-growing story.Business was bustling at Bobby's lemonade stand, but Mr. Vozar knew that maintaining a small-town feel would be Bobby's next big challenge as the business grew. He sat Bobby down under the shade of an old oak tree that stood like a sentinel beside the stand. 'Bobby, your lemonade is a hit. But remember, as you grow, you'll need to balance efficiency with that personal touch which brings people back.' Bobby nodded intently, his notebook at the ready.

The first idea that Bobby developed was to create a 'Flavor of the Month' campaign. Each month, Bobby would introduce a new flavor, utilizing fresh, seasonal ingredients and seeking feedback from his customers to engage them in the business. This would allow customers to feel like they were part of the business's growth, not just passive consumers. September's Apple Cider Lemonade, with a dash of cinnamon, became a quick favorite, solidifying Bobby's reputation for innovation.

To bolster word-of-mouth, he started a loyalty program – 'Bobby's Lemon Circle'. For every ten cups purchased, customers would get one free, and they would also receive a lemonade-themed badge after each milestone. These badges became a badge of honor among the local kids, who eagerly showcased them on backpacks and jackets. 'Mr. Vozar, look how many people come back just to show off their new badges!' Bobby exclaimed with amazement.

'Earned media' was another term Mr. Vozar taught Bobby. He suggested that Bobby reach out to the local paper, and soon enough, the 'Daily Squeeze' was featuring heartwarming stories about the lemonade stand. These drew people from all over town and even from neighboring areas who were curious about the lemonade stand that made front-page news.

But Bobby knew that marketing wasn't just about attracting new customers; it was about keeping them too. So he made sure that every glass served was accompanied with the same warm smile and chat about their day. He taught his new employee, Julie, that the stories customers shared were just as important as the lemonade they sipped. As the summer heat persisted, even the mayor stopped by for his regular 'Mayor's Mint Medley' and couldn't help but rave about it on his social media, boosting Bobby's business further.As Julie poured another round of lemonade, she marveled at how the stand had transformed. It had only been a few weeks since Mr. Vozar had shared his business acumen with Bobby, but the results were staggering. After taking Mr. Vozar's lessons to heart, Bobby had overhauled his marketing strategy, turning an overlooked street corner into a buzzing center of community activity.

When the Flavor of the Month campaign was announced, a palpable buzz had arisen around 'Luscious Lavender Lemonade'. Parents with strollers, teenagers on skateboards, and couples on leisurely walks made their way to Bobby's stand to taste the novel flavor that had been inspired by Mrs. Kinley's garden down the street. Everyone was excited to see what the next month would bring.

In tandem, Bobby's Lemon Circle loyalty program encouraged repeat customers. Bobby's booth now displayed a poster with a giant lemon that had a punch-out circle for each purchase; ten punches promised a free lemonade, and customers eagerly presented their cards with each visit, excited to inch closer to their complimentary treat.

Success also meant new opportunities and challenges. Bobby realized he needed to maintain the personal touch that had become a hallmark of his stand as the business grew. He wondered aloud to Mr. Vozar if adding new flavors was enough or if more services, like a delivery option, might be attractive to his customers.

'Diversification can be good, Bobby, but remember to stay true to your roots. Your customers love the simplicity and authenticity of your lemonade,' Mr. Vozar advised during one of their regular mentorship meetings.

Bobby also started hearing the term 'franchising' being tossed around by excited neighbors. 'Imagine, Bobby,' said Mr. Jenkins, sipping the last of his peach lemonade, 'you could have stands all across the country!' The idea was tempting, but also daunting.

Bobby jotted down notes on franchising, flipping through pages of his now well-worn business primer. Mr. Vozar had told him, 'A franchise requires systems, training, and a keen understanding of scaling.' Bobby wasn't sure if he was ready, but he was hungry to learn more.

As summer waned, the framework of Bobby's bigger dreams began to take shape, subtly altering the landscape of his youthful ambitions.Summer's embrace began to loosen, and with it, the natural flux of customers started to ebb. But for Bobby Lemons, the dwindling crowd wasn't a sign of defeat; it was an opportunity to strategize. Noting each dip and swell in his business with the precision of a seasoned entrepreneur, Bobby welcomed the change as a challenge.

With Mr. Vozar's guidance, he embarked on a journey to understand the heart of his growing business—the brand. 'Bobby, my boy,' Mr. Vozar would often start, balancing the gravity of his teachings with the warmth of his smile, 'the strength of your lemonade isn't just in its taste, but in the story it tells. Your brand is your promise to your customers.'

Under this new canopy of knowledge, Bobby began experimenting with innovative marketing tactics. He initiated a 'Create Your Own Flavor' contest, inviting his customers to concoct their lemonade flavors with the winner featured for a week. Children and adults alike flooded in, eager to mix, test, and name their creations. The contest didn't just add a tang of excitement—it cultivated a sense of community around Bobby's Lemonade Stand.

He also dabbled in social media, with his friends helping to set up accounts on various platforms. Before long, photos of vibrant lemonade glasses frosted with condensation were shared and liked, reaching an audience far beyond the neighborhood. Bobby knew the power of these pixilated realms—as he had learned, word-of-mouth in the digital age could be just as potent as the neighborly chatter over backyard fences.

Lemonade Stand's warm autumn hues mirrored Bobby's optimistic atmosphere. As he finalized another day's accounts, he mused over the future. The whispers of franchising, like a distant melody, played compellingly in his mind. The process was complex, surely, but its potential was as ripe and vivid as the lemons that catalyzed his venture. Bobby decided that the following day, he would make a list of questions to ask Mr. Vozar. It was time to prepare for the journey ahead, and questions were the compass by which he would navigate. As the sun set, painting the sky with streaks of orange and pink, Bobby felt a surge of determination. The stand had taught him much, but he was ready to step beyond and chase the horizon of his dreams.

Standing behind his bright yellow stand the next morning, Bobby watched as regulars approached with smiles, expecting their usual refreshing drink. The 'Create Your Own Flavor' contest had been a hit, creating a buzz that even the local newspaper caught wind of, resulting a feature story that further spread the word about his unique lemonade stand. The article was shared on social media, and suddenly, Bobby Lemons became a small-town sensation.

Never had he imagined that his little stand could gain such attention. People from neighboring areas began showing up, eager to sample the winning flavor—a delightful mix of lemon, cucumber, and mint, aptly named 'Cucumber Breeze'. Bobby's social media accounts were aflutter with activity, as customers posted selfies with their lemonade cups alongside the hashtag #LemonadeInnovator. Bobby reaped the rewards of word-of-mouth marketing, learning that a good product paired with exceptional customer experience was the best advertisement.

As his lemonade stand grew busier by the day, Bobby felt a swell of pride. Yet with the increased interest, he wondered how he could maintain the quality and personal touch that had made his stand so beloved if he were to franchise. These thoughts gripped him as he prepared his pitcher of lemonade, each squeeze of the lemon stirring reflections on his next steps.

However, beyond marketing strategies and customer engagement, a pressing concern remained: scale. To keep up with the demand without losing the charm of his brand, Bobby needed a solid plan. While juggling the steady stream of customers, he managed to jot down questions for Mr. Vozar on a sticky note that soon was filled with his tight, meticulous handwriting.

The day waned, and as the customers dwindled, Bobby pulled down the stand's striped awning and lined his questions up neatly. First thing after school tomorrow, he decided, he would seek the counsel of Mr. Vozar. The sun dipped low, and just like the day it first burst into light, his little lemonade stand glowed under the twilight, a beacon of his burgeoning dreams.

First Signs of Success

As the following morning painted the sky in shades of pink and orange, Bobby was already behind his stand before most of his peers had even rubbed the sleep from their eyes. It wasn't just the promise of an early customer or two that brought him out of bed while the dew was still fresh on the grass; Bobby was animated by the thought of showing Mr. Vozar his progress and seeking his advice for the future.

The stand was now a well-oiled machine, running with efficiency that would make a seasoned entrepreneur nod with approval. Bobby checked the stock of fresh lemons, ice, and sugar, ensuring the day's operations would run smoothly without interruption. As the neighborhood began to stir, a handful of regulars queued up, their morning routines now happily intertwined with Bobby's tangy concoction. The laughter and chattering around the stand had become background music to his enterprise, creating an atmosphere as refreshing as the lemonade he served.

However, with popularity came challenges. Bobby noticed the need for a better queue system because customers were crowding around the stand, sometimes blocking the sidewalk. Drawing upon what Mr. Vozar had told him about customer service, he quickly sketched a more organized line system using chalk on the concrete and placed friendly 'Stand Here' signs, smiling as he saw the immediate positive reaction from his patrons.

By midday, Bobby's eyes flickered between his customers and the clock - it was nearly time to visit Mr. Vozar. He found it harder to step away from the stand now that business was bustling, fearing that his absence might cause a dip in his hard-earned momentum. But he knew that the insight he could gain from Mr. Vozar might be crucial to sustaining that momentum in the long run.

Gathering the sticky note from beneath the cash register where he had secured it, Bobby brushed his hands off on his apron and locked the cash drawer. He entrusted the stand to Mrs. Jenkins, a loyal customer who had volunteered to help whenever he had business matters to attend to. With gratitude, Bobby sprinted off toward the school, the anticipation of his upcoming consultation mixing with the bubbling excitement in his chest. The warmth of the summer sun beat down on Bobby's back as he jogged towards the school, his mind racing with thoughts as brisk as his steps. With each block he covered, his confidence swelled like the juice sacs of a ripe lemon. He was eager to present his progress to Mr. Vozar and more importantly, to absorb his wisdom on expanding this small venture into something resembling the beginnings of an empire.

As he rounded the corner to the school's main entrance, Bobby took a moment to wipe the sweat from his brow and straighten his apron, now adorned with the logo he and Mr. Vozar had brainstormed—a smiling cartoon lemon, tipping its hat, which became an endearing symbol of Bobby's stand. The doors loomed in front of him, surprisingly daunting despite the countless times he'd passed through them. This time, it was different. He wasn't a student with a backpack this time; he was an entrepreneur with a mission. It gave him a sense of purpose he had never felt in these halls before.

Mr. Vozar was waiting for him in the usual room, Room 102, where the world of business had first been unfurled to Bobby. The room smelt faintly of chalk and the promise of young minds yearning for knowledge. Only today, it was just Bobby and Mr. Vozar, spread across a desk littered with charts, graphs, and the lemonade business plan they had nurtured together.

'Bobby! Look at you, a businessman in his prime!' Mr. Vozar, with his tweed jacket and warm, encouraging smile, greeted him with a hearty handshake. 'So, tell me, how has our little enterprise been faring?'

Bobby took a deep breath and plunged into the details. Customers were up, sales were steady, and the buzz about his lemonade was growing. Yet, he spoke mostly of the excitement he found himself engulfed in—the constant hum of chatter around the stand, the thrill of seeing regulars return, and the pride of being able to hire his first employee, even if it was just for a few hours a week.

'But Mr. Vozar,' Bobby concluded, 'the stand is more than I ever hoped it could be, but I feel like I'm at capacity. How do I go bigger without losing what made Bobby's Lemons special in the first place?'Mr. Vozar looked at Bobby with a warm, understanding smile. He motioned for him to sit down at a small round table in the corner of Room 102, where a chess club had left behind a board with an unfinished game still in play. 'Bobby,' he began, wiping his glasses on his tie before putting them back on, 'what you're talking about is scaling up, and that, my young entrepreneur, is a delicate dance between growth and quality.' Bobby nodded, absorbing every word like a sponge.

'To begin with,' Mr. Vozar continued, tapping a chess piece thoughtfully, 'you might consider opening a second stand, but to do that effectively, you'll need to replicate the essence of what made the first one successful. That means having a consistent product, reliable service, and... your unique charm.' Bobby jotted down notes vigorously, his pencil barely keeping up with his thoughts. 'But that's where a franchise model can come into play,' Mr. Vozar added. 'It allows for expansion, while still maintaining a uniform standard across all locations.' Bobby's eyes widened with curiosity at the mention of franchising, a concept entirely new to him.

'Maintenance of quality is paramount, Bobby. When franchises falter, it's often because their product becomes inconsistent. You'll need systems in place, comprehensive training for your franchisees, and perhaps most importantly, regular quality checks.' Mr. Vozar spoke with an authority that only years of experience could grant. He went on to explain the intricacies of franchise agreements, trademarking, and the importance of choosing the right partners who would share Bobby's vision and values.

As their meeting drew to a close, Bobby felt a surging sense of purpose. He thanked Mr. Vozar profusely and headed back to his lemonade stand, his mind brimming with ideas. The next several weeks were a blur of activity for Bobby. He revised his recipes to ensure they could be easily replicated, created an operations manual to capture the Bobby's Lemons' way, and even developed a training program for his prospective franchisees. Each step felt like a monumental leap toward his dreams.

The stand had never been busier. Bobby implemented a new point-of-sale system to handle the increased transactions and made minute adjustments to the layout to improve customer flow. He was everywhere at once, greeting customers, overseeing his new employee, and always maintaining that unique Bobby's touch. The excitement was palpable, and the community buzzed with anticipation of what Bobby's Lemons would become next. The sun glared down with unrelenting intensity, but Bobby Lemons felt nothing but the cool breeze of success fluttering through his stand. With every freshly squeezed glass, his confidence swelled. Learning the ins and outs of the lemonade business from Mr. Vozar had been transformative, and now the fruits of his labor were as sweet as the lemonade he served.

His once shaky enterprise had morphed into a well-oiled machine. Customers lined up, enticed by the vibrant new banner flaunting 'Bobby's Best!' that hung cheerfully above the stand. The local newspaper even featured a small piece on the entrepreneurial spirit of Bobby, and that only fanned the flames of curiosity in the town. Word of mouth became Bobby's best ally as the stand's fame spread like wildfire.

In the thick of the hustle, Bobby found himself faced with the challenges of success. He learned to juggle inventories, ensuring he never ran out of fresh lemons or sugar. The notion of cost of goods sold (COGS) was no longer just a concept but a practical target to hit each day. As the sun began to wane, he tallied up the day's earnings, feeling a surge of pride as he recorded the revenue and gross profit, intimately aware of each expense that factored into his net profit.

One particularly sweltering afternoon, a small group of students from the local high school approached the stand, their eyes filled with admiration and curiosity. 'We're studying small businesses in Economics class, and we heard about your success. Could we interview you for our project?' they asked earnestly. Bobby, never one to miss an opportunity to inspire others, agreed with a wide grin.

Amid answering questions about his business strategies and marketing efforts, Bobby realized he was becoming a role model in the community. It wasn't just about lemonade anymore – it was about inspiring others and leaving an impact. The interview went splendidly, and the students left with a newfound appreciation for the intricacies of running a business. Bobby couldn't help but feel a twinge of nostalgia, thinking back to his early days of confusion before Mr. Vozar extended his guiding hand.

As dusk settled in, the rush started to die down, and Bobby finally had a moment to catch his breath. The stand had been successful beyond his wildest dreams, but he knew he couldn't rest on his laurels. There was more to do, more to achieve. Preparations for expansion and finding the right franchisees were looming on the horizon, and Bobby was eager to embark on this new chapter. With a sparkle in his eyes and a mind brimming with ideas, he jotted down notes for scouting locations for his second stand, ensuring they would align with his vision for Bobby's Lemons – fresh, vibrant, and full of community spirit. With the hum of activity around him, Bobby's mind raced with excitement and a touch of anxiety. The lemonade stand was now more than just a small summer project—it was the seedling of what could be a thriving business. His lemonade, which had started out with a very local and modest reach, was now a hit. The increase in sales and a growing customer base brought new challenges though. His inventory needed careful management, and with the uptick in sales, shortages were a regular worry.

To combat this, Bobby initiated a simple inventory tracking system. He used a whiteboard to mark the comings and goings of supplies, ensuring that he always had enough lemons, sugar, and cups on hand. The days of guessing and last-minute shopping trips were over. He set up alerts with local suppliers, negotiating better prices for bulk purchases. These were the lessons from Mr. Vozar, paying off in real-time.

The newfound popularity of his stand didn't go unnoticed. One sweltering Saturday, a crowd formed a line that snaked around the corner. Bobby was sweating not just from the heat, but also from the pressure to keep up with the demands. He had friends helping, but even that was becoming too little manpower for the growing business. He knew he needed more hands, and maybe more stands.

Curiosity about his success spread to local high school students who were fascinated by this mini entrepreneur. Bobby did not keep his secrets to himself and offered them a candid interview, detailing the intricacies of running a profitable lemonade business. His story sparked a flame of entrepreneurship within the community. Teens spoke of starting their own ventures, looking up to Bobby as a role model.

Amidst managing these exciting developments, Bobby also started exploring the idea of expansion more seriously. He dedicated his mornings to looking for ideal locations for a second stand. He considered foot traffic, nearby competition, and community engagement. The weekends were for visiting potential sites and imagining a new, vibrant lemonade stand—another beacon of friendly service and refreshing beverages.

Entrepreneurial spirit fueled Bobby's days and nights. The challenges brought on by success taught him invaluable lessons of growth, sustainability, and community integration. Every sip sold was not just a transaction; it was an exchange of his childhood dream materializing into a reality that was palpable. As the chapter of his venture drew to a close that Sunday evening, Bobby looked at his stand—a stand that was no longer just his, but a part of the community. It was a symbol of what a little knowledge, a lot of passion, and a sprinkle of sugar could achieve.Bobby awoke the next morning with a sense of purpose that was almost palpable. He had done the math; his lemonade stand, once a humble enterprise, was now a harbinger of a potential empire. But he knew that to grow further, he needed to find the perfect spot for his second location—a place with enough foot traffic to guarantee a steady stream of thirsty customers. After meticulous research and several scouting trips around town, Bobby found a prime spot near the local park, which was bustling with families on weekends and had ample parking. Excitement filled his chest as he began formulating plans for his next big move.

With the daily operations at his current stand running smoothly, Bobby started crafting a blueprint for his franchise model. He consulted books, absorbed advice from Mr. Vozar, and even reached out to local business owners for their insights. While the intricacies of partnership structures and legalities were complex and sometimes dizzying, Bobby felt an energizing thrill with each new piece of the puzzle he fit into place. 'This has to be foolproof,' he thought to himself, 'A model that others can replicate and succeed with.'

Simultaneously, as his business acumen sharpened, the demand for his lemonade soared. Sun-kissed kids on skateboards made a pit stop at Bobby's stand, construction workers sauntered over for a refreshing break, and even the mail carriers made it a point to schedule their routes around a midday lemonade break. With this growth, Bobby faced logistical challenges. He needed to streamline his supply chain to avoid running out of lemons or ice, which had happened on one sweltering Friday, resulting in lost sales and some disappointed customers.

Realizing that a busier stand also meant more responsibility and potential for error, Bobby carefully crafted a contingency plan. He delegated certain tasks to his most trustworthy friends, who were more than happy to help in exchange for a free glass of lemonade or a small stipend. It was a win-win; Bobby could focus on expansion plans while ensuring his stand operated without a hitch.

By the end of the week, Bobby had drafted the outlines of a franchise agreement and operational manual. He knew that selecting the right franchisees would be critical for maintaining the quality and spirit of his brand. As the sun dipped below the horizon, he sat back in his chair, exhausted yet exhilarated. He had transformed from a boy with a small lemonade stand to an entrepreneur with big dreams and the drive to match. But there was still much to do before his dreams of a franchise would come to fruition. For now, he was content with the progress made and the promise of a bright and busy tomorrow.Even though the day was winding down, Bobby's lemonade stand was still abuzz with customers. The location near the park seemed like a masterstroke—the foot traffic was a marketer's dream come true. Families returning from their evening walks, joggers looking to quench their thirst, and groups of teenagers gravitating towards the stand as if it was the new local hangout spot.

All this activity, however, brought with it a new set of challenges. Bobby found himself multitasking more than ever. He poured lemonade with one hand while restocking cups with the other. He engaged with customers, calling out playful greetings and answering questions about his secret recipe, all while keeping an eye on inventory levels. It was a juggling act that required wit, agility, and staying power. The stand had grown busier than he had ever imagined. Kids from the neighborhood wanted to lend a hand, seeing the lemonade stand as an exciting venture rather than mere child's play. Bobby, embracing his newfound role as a leader and teacher, began instructing them on the art of lemonade making and the basics of customer service.

One balmy evening, as a line formed that stretched around the corner, Bobby heard laughter and chatter about the famous 'Lemonade Mogul'—a title the locals had affectionately bestowed upon him. The whispers of expansion were in the air, and the community was eager to see Bobby succeed. 'Lemon by lemon, stand by stand,' he thought to himself, allowing a grin to grow across his face. Nevertheless, amidst the excitement, he managed to keep his focus on the numbers, tracking every sale and calculating the day's profits after the park had emptied and the stand was closed.

Bobby knew that a successful business required more than just high spirits and bustling trade—it needed sound financial management and strategic planning. That night, as he counted the day's takings, he realized that his dreams were slowly but surely turning into reality. Success was no longer just a distant fantasy but a tangible achievement that was growing, just like the lines at his stand.

Expanding the Menu

The early days of Bobby Lemons' lemonade stand were now a distant memory overshadowed by the vibrant energy of success. The aroma of fresh lemons and the smiles from satisfied customers were a testament to Bobby's hard work. But, as Mr. Vozar would often remind him, 'Success is not a destination, but a journey that requires constant innovation.' Taking this to heart, Bobby decided it was time to expand his offerings, hoping to keep his loyal customers intrigued and attract new ones.

On a particularly bright Saturday morning, Bobby set up a small 'Lab' table next to his regular stand, displaying an array of new and exciting flavors. The 'Lemons Lab'—as he endearingly called it—featured lemonade flavors infused with raspberries, peaches, mint, and even a spicy ginger kick. Bobby understood the risks of product diversification; it required meticulous inventory tracking and could potentially increase his COGS if not managed properly. But with Mr. Vozar's teachings in mind, he was careful to calculate his anticipated expenses and set prices that would keep his profits healthy.

As the word spread about the new flavors, kids and adults alike would line up, curious and eager to try the latest concoctions from the Lemons Lab. Each feedback was precious, and Bobby began to understand customer preferences and seasonal trends. He also learned the importance of managing stock and minimizing waste; for instance, seeing the mint flavor's popularity soar on hot days, he would prepare extra, while ginger lemonade, a surprising hit, became a permanent weekend specialty.

Experimenting wasn't without its hiccups, though. A batch of blueberry lemonade didn't resonate as expected, and Bobby had to figure out what to do with the leftover stock. It was a lesson in adaptability and reacting to market demands. With Mr. Vozar's guidance, he turned the setback into a learning opportunity, developing a 'Mix Your Own' option where adventurous customers could blend flavors. The idea was a hit, adding an interactive element to his business, and saved the blueberry lemonade from going to waste.

Bobby's ledger became more complex but also more rewarding. Each evening, as he recorded the daily transactions, he would examine which flavors were hits and which needed tweaking or promoting. Marketing, another vital lesson from Mr. Vozar, came into play as Bobby used social media to announce flavor releases and created a loyalty program for his customer base. It wasn't long before nearby businesses noticed and approached Bobby for potential partnerships.

As the chapter of evolution drew to a close, Bobby's original little lemonade stand had become a community hotspot, a hub of refreshing flavors, and a showcase of a young entrepreneur's blossoming ambition. His dreams were materializing, one cup at a time.Summer rolled in with a generous shine, and Bobby Lemons found himself amidst a blend of opportunities and challenges. The increased foot traffic meant more taste buds to satisfy and a need for quicker service. Bobby, eyeing his goals, wasn't one to back down. After meticulous research and taste-tests with his friends, Bobby introduced a new line-up of exotic twists: Blueberry Bliss, Watermelon Whirl, and his personal favorite, Mango Madness.

On top of that, he toyed with the idea of 'Special of the Day' to keep customers guessing and excited for what's coming next. It became an instant hit, and regulars started to plan their visits around these daily surprises. But with every new creation, the complexity of his operations grew. Managing stock became a jigsaw puzzle; too much of one ingredient meant potential waste, while too little could lead to disappointed customers. Bobby learned the art of forecasting, adjusting his orders based on weather predictions, local events, and past sales data.

On exceptionally hot days, he started serving 'Frozen Lemon Zesties', which became a sensation among the kids. It was a playful twist that also addressed the excess stock of lemons he occasionally had. Nothing went to waste, as Bobby mastered the act of transforming surplus into opportunity.

He trialed a referral program, incentivizing his young customers with freebies for bringing in friends or posting about their lemonade experience online. Not surprisingly, word-of-mouth spread like wildfire, and the stand saw a new wave of lemonade enthusiasts. Expanding further, Bobby partnered with local bakeries, offering complimentary pastries with his lemonades. It not only solved the bakeries' issue of unsold inventory but also enhanced his customers' experience.

As the summer days stretched on and the stand's fame grew, Bobby realized he was sitting at the cusp of something bigger than just a summer gig. His sights were set on a vision now vivid in its attainability – his very own franchise and the seedling of a lemonade empire. He knew the journey ahead would be stringent with learning curves, but with Mr. Vozar's wisdom echoing in his resolve, Bobby Lemons was ready for the next leap.Behind Bobby's stand, an assortment of fresh fruits now adorned the counter, a colorful testament to his expanding menu. With each lemonade flavor sporting a quirky name like 'Razzle-Dazzle Raspberry' or 'Minty Meadow Melody', customers couldn't help but stop by, tempted by the novelty. But Bobby wasn't content with just catchy titles - he spent evenings experimenting with ratios and ingredients, determined to perfect each concoction.

One balmy afternoon, a customer suggested, "You know what would be great? A spicy lemonade!" The idea sparked a light in Bobby's eyes. That weekend, he unveiled 'Sizzling Citrus Surprise', a blend with just enough kick to intrigue the bravest taste buds. It was an instant hit, and Bobby learned an invaluable lesson - to listen and respond to customer feedback.

Bobby's newfound attention to detail and quality didn't go unnoticed. A local food blogger stumbled upon the stand and was so impressed with the variety and taste that she wrote a glowing review. Word of mouth spread like wildfire, and soon people from neighboring towns were visiting, eager to quench their curiosity along with their thirst.

The influx of customers meant Bobby had to refine his inventory management. Restocking fruits, and keeping track of sales for each flavor became a daily ritual. He created charts and graphs, tracking the rise and fall of each product's popularity, and adjusted his purchases accordingly. This not only reduced waste but also boosted his net profits.

Bobby was careful to maintain the homey charm that brought him initial fame; he made sure that with every tweak and innovation, the core experience - a refreshing glass of homemade lemonade - remained unchanged. With the busy hum of content customers mingling with the clinking of ice cubes, Bobby felt a swell of pride. The lemonade stand was no longer just a fixture on the sidewalk; it was a destination.

As the sun dipped below the horizon, painting the sky in shades of orange and pink, Bobby began to close up shop. He meticulously counted the day's earnings, recorded the remaining inventory, and jotted down ideas for the next special flavor. Today was a good day, but tomorrow, he sensed, could be even better. With the guidance of Mr. Vozar and an innate business acumen burgeoning within, he was inching ever closer to the fruits of his labor becoming the seeds of his future lemonade kingdom.A brisk breeze whistled through the trees as Bobby finally locked up his cash box and covered his lemonade stand. His day's reflections were interrupted by the sound of his own name. Turning around, he was greeted by Mr. Vozar, who was walking his little terrier, Mr. Spritz. 'Another day at the helm, Bobby?' Mr. Vozar asked cheerfully, his eyes twinkling behind his rounded glasses. Bobby grinned, 'Just closed, but it was a great day. The new flavors are a hit!' His teacher's smile widened, 'I see your experiments are paying off. Keep being innovative; it's key to staying ahead.'

Encouraged by Mr. Vozar's words, Bobby spent the evening in his makeshift kitchen lab, browsing through cookbooks and online recipes for inspiration. He concocted new lemonade variations, infusing them with locally sourced honey, mint from his backyard, and even a hint of lavender. The process was experimental, thrilling, and sometimes a little messy, but by late night, he had crafted several new contenders poised to refresh the palates of his loyal customers.

The next morning, Bobby unveiled 'Bee's Knees Lemon Squeeze' and 'Minty Fresh Mystery' at the stand. The former, with its sweet and floral notes, was an immediate enchantress; the latter, a refreshing burst, equally captivated. Customers would sip tentatively, then their eyes would light up, a nod and a smile would ensue, and Bobby knew he had another hit. As he witnessed their reactions, he also realized the importance of capturing these moments. So, he asked his friend, Eliza, who was dabbing in photography, to take candid shots of customers enjoying his creations.

Bobby soon displayed these genuine moments of joy by his lemonade stand, adding a personal touch that transcended the typical advertisements seen around town. To keep his customers engaged, he also introduced 'Lemonade of the Week,' which invited his regulars to come back for something new routinely.

Days turned into weeks, and a rhythm to his business began to emerge. Stocking, creating, and selling became like clockwork. The buzz around Bobby's lemonade stand grew, and with each new flavor, a fresh wave of customers arrived. With his newfound understanding of managing a product line, Bobby started to document each flavor's popularity. He began to notice patterns – how weather, local events, and even the day of the week affected his sales. This insight allowed him to forecast demand more accurately, manage his inventory, and reduce waste. It was a delicate balance, one that Bobby found both challenging and rewarding.

As summer reached its zenith, so did the popularity of Bobby Lemons' lemonade stand. He realized that to maintain this momentum, he needed to keep innovating, but also stabilize the product line that had become his foundation. His unique flavors were a cornerstone of his brand, and he needed to ensure they couldn't be easily replicated. To protect his intellectual property, he sought advice from Mr. Vozar on obtaining trademarks for his most popular concoctions. Mr. Vozar, who wasn't just a business teacher but also had a law degree, guided Bobby through the basics of intellectual property law, emphasizing the importance of protecting his brand as part of his business strategy.

The journey from a simple lemonade stand to a burgeoning business had been swift yet abundant with lessons. Bobby knew his next step was crucial, and soon he would have to face the realm of franchising, a path sprinkled with legal complexities and the need for strategic planning. As he covered the stand that evening, under the starlit sky, thoughts of lemonade stands sprouting in other neighborhoods filled his mind with dreams and an unfaltering determination. 'Tomorrow,' he whispered to the stars, 'we plan for an even bigger future.'Chapter 8

As summer's warm embrace intensified, so did the clamor of customers at Bobby Lemon's stand. The fragrance of fresh lemons fused with the aroma of new, exciting flavors, creating a symphony of scents that tickled the palates of eager patrons. Bobby was more than just a lemonade seller now; he was a craftsman of refreshment, an architect of taste.

He rigorously tested his new concoctions - strawberry-lemonade for the sweet tooth, cucumber-mint for a refreshing twist, and even a sassy ginger-spiked variety. Each new flavor required careful calculation and resource management, something Mr. Vozar called 'Product Line Evolution.' The variety didn't just offer a novelty; it kept the stand lustrous in the eyes of repeat customers thirsty for new experiences.

With Mr. Vozar's guidance, Bobby learned to track which flavors were hits and which were misses by tallying up sales and collecting customer feedback. The data painted a vivid picture - while keeping his classic lemonade as the stalwart anchor, Bobby adjusted his offerings like a seasoned market analyst. He introduced a 'Flavor of the Week' to test small batches, limiting risk while eliciting excitement.

One particular scorching Saturday, as the queue snaked around the corner, a thought struck Bobby. 'Why not turn these recipes into products people can take home?' With a sparkle in his eye, Bobby shared his idea with Mr. Vozar, who was nodding approvingly, sipping a lavender-infused pink lemonade.

'Make-your-own-lemonade kits, brilliant!' Mr. Vozar exclaimed, 'You're thinking like a true entrepreneur, Bobby. It's about creating value that extends beyond the stand. Let's draft a plan to include costs, packaging, and distribution.'

The rest of the summer season was dedicated to perfecting this new branch of products. Bobby worked on the designs for the packaging, making sure it was as bright and sunny as his stand. They sourced high-quality, yet affordable components: custom measuring spoons, recipe cards with his secret mixes, pre-measured sugar packets, and even a special Lemonade Stand League membership card for repeat buyers.

Sales were blooming like the flowers in Mrs. Greenspan's garden. Children from all around the neighborhood were starting to talk about the 'Lemonade Stand League' and how they wanted to be part of Bobby's crew. The kits became immensely popular, parents loved the idea of a teachable moment in the form of a refreshing beverage, and kids were thrilled to mix their own drinks at home.

As Bobby tallied up the final day's earnings before school resumed, there was a triumphant sparkle in his eye. The stand had taught him the sweet taste of success, but it had also given him a thirst for further achievements. With summer waving its last golden rays goodbye, Bobby knew he had harvested enough experience and confidence to take the next step. The world of franchising awaited, with its daunting promise of growth and the challenge of reproducing success. 'I'm ready,' he murmured, as he turned the 'Open' sign off one last time for the season.

Building a Brand

As fall approached, the leaves started to don hues of auburn and gold, painting a vibrant backdrop for Bobby Lemons' latest venture. Turning that 'Open' sign off was no swan song; it was a clarion call to greater endeavors. Peering through his now-familiar pitcher-shaped window, Bobby mused over how far he had come since that first lukewarm day of sales. With a smile, however, he came to realize that to carve out his own slice of the lemonade market, his stand needed something more—a spark of singular vitality.

'Mr. Vozar,' Bobby started one cool afternoon, their sessions evolving from makeshift classrooms to strategy forums, 'I think we need to make my lemonade stand... \'unmistakably Bobby\\". His eyebrows knitted together as he pondered. 'We need branding!'

The mention of that term brought a gleeful glint to Mr. Vozar's eyes. 'Exactly, Bobby! Branding gives your business a memorable identity. It's not just about what you sell, but how people perceive what you sell,' he explained. They dug into discussions, Mr. Vozar's kitchen scattered with branding books and magazines. 'Your brand should reflect your product's identity, your values, and the message you want to convey to your customers,' Mr. Vozar elaborated while sipping on a glass of Bobby's original lemonade concoction.

Bobby's brain churned with ideas. 'What about... Bobby's Sunshine Sips?' he ventured.

Mr. Vozar smiled approvingly. 'It's personable, it's happy, it's... sunny. But let's refine it, Bobby. Think simplicity. Brand names that linger are often punchy and straightforward.'

They set to work, erasing and rewriting on the large whiteboard until finally, the perfect blend of words materialized, and 'Lemons by Bobby' was born. It suggested quality, a personal touch,

and an obvious nod to the lemon-filled heritage they were
cultivating.

Next was the logo. It had to be as refreshing and distinctive
as the lemonade itself. 'Remember, your logo is often the first
introduction to your brand. Make it count,' Mr. Vozar iterated as
they sketched various designs.

Bobby was lost in concentration when the idea struck him. 'It
should be a lemon, but not just any lemon—a lemon wearing
sunglasses!' The symbol of cool perfectly personified the youthful
spirit of his burgeoning enterprise.

With Mr. Vozar's guidance, they fashioned a sleek, stylized
lemon adorned with cool shades. It was simple, yet whimsically
sharp—a true embodiment of 'Lemons by Bobby.' The brand was
poised to radiate warmth and zest, much like the summer sun under
which its foundation had been poured.

Bobby was invigorated, but he knew the path ahead was
lined with more than just citrusy aspirations. It was time to
understand the intricacies of franchising, grasp the legal bonds that
would hold his dreams in reality, and strategize for establishing his
second lemonade stand. As he helped Mr. Vozar wipe the
whiteboard clean, Bobby felt a rush of anticipation for the road
ahead, where 'Lemons by Bobby' would soon quench the thirst of
countless more.As the leaves turned golden and began to fall,
revealing the bare bones of the trees, Bobby's lemonade stand stood
silent and empty. The once bustling corner of Maple Avenue and
Fourth Street was now just a memory of summer. But within the
quiet space of Mr. Vozar's classroom, ideas and plans bloomed like
spring flowers.

'Mr. Vozar, how do we start? I mean, franchising feels huge,'
said Bobby, with a mixture of excitement and trepidation painting
his words.

'That's a good question, Bobby. Think of franchising as cloning your lemonade stand, but there's a lot to consider. First, you'll need an operations manual,' Mr. Vozar explained, his glasses perched precariously on the edge of his nose. 'It's the DNA of your business. It details how to run the stand, make the lemonade, serve the customers – everything the way you do it, so that every 'Lemons by Bobby' feels like the original.'

Bobby nodded keenly, absorbing every word like a sponge. 'What about the legal stuff?' he asked, aware that this was a territory far removed from juicing lemons and mixing sugar.

'Ah, yes, legalities. You'll need a franchise attorney to help draft your franchise agreement and other required documents. These will lay out the terms under which you'll allow franchisees to operate under the 'Lemons by Bobby' brand,' replied Mr. Vozar, turning to the whiteboard to sketch out the basic framework of these documents.

There was a whole new vocabulary to learn – franchise fees, royalty payments, marketing funds. Terms that seemed daunting, but with Mr. Vozar's patient explanations, they began to fit into place like pieces of a puzzle.

'Your success can be replicated, Bobby. But you must ensure that your franchisees share your passion, commitment, and – most importantly – the quality that has made 'Lemons by Bobby' a local favorite,' Mr. Vozar continued, emphasizing the importance of selecting the right people to carry the brand forward.

Bobby's mind buzzed with questions. Would people be interested in buying a franchise? How would he market this opportunity? And how would he maintain the quality and culture of 'Lemons by Bobby' across multiple stands? Mr. Vozar saw the worry lines etch into Bobby's forehead and reassured him, 'One step at a time, Bobby. Rome wasn't built in a day, and neither is a successful franchise.'

They spent the next weeks delving deeper into the process. Bobby drafted the first version of his operations manual, a blueprint that captured his methods and values. He began networking, shaking hands with local business owners, and learning the essence of making connections. With each new lesson, his confidence grew, and the brand 'Lemons by Bobby' began to feel less like a dream and more like the vibrant, viable business it was destined to become.

As fall surrendered to the chill of winter, Bobby embraced the learning curve, realizing that every ice-covered branch and quiet snowy morning brought him closer to reinventing his lemonade stand for the spring.Beneath the watchful eye of Mr. Vozar, Bobby began to weave the various threads of his education into a cohesive tapestry. The first step was cementing the brand identity of 'Lemons by Bobby'. They had brainstormed a range of names, but it was the simplicity and personal touch of this one that felt just right. 'People should know there's a young, dedicated person behind their refreshment,' Mr. Vozar had advised. And so, with a name decided, they worked on a logo that was both eye-catching and resonant with the values of the enterprise. After numerous sketches and revisions, they settled on a whimsical lemon with a broad smile, wearing sunglasses and a crown of leaves. The slogan below it read: 'Fresh Royalty - Reigning over thirst, one lemon at a time.'

Bobby felt a sense of pride every time he looked at the new banner hanging above his stand, feeling that it truly signified what he wanted his business to represent. The logo was plastered across all his social media, business cards, and the menus.

As 'Lemons by Bobby' was now visually represented, it was time to build upon the foundations they had set and find people who were willing to buy into Bobby's vision and spread the fresh taste of his lemonade far and wide. Winter, though usually a time of hibernation for lemonade enterprises, became Bobby's season of growth. He dove into developing a training program that would encapsulate everything 'Lemons by Bobby' stood for. It wasn't enough to simply show future franchisees how to make lemonade; they needed to be taught how to stir in that same generosity and community spirit that Bobby and Mr. Vozar had grated into the brand's zest.

Walking along the snow-tipped streets, Bobby visited other successful franchises, taking notes on their operations. He asked questions about their training processes, how they ensured consistency across different locations, and what made their customer service stand out. He compiled his findings into a training handbook, a companion piece to the operations manual, replete with quizzes, checklists, and training schedules—everything a new owner would need to keep the 'Lemons by Bobby' ethos alive.

His next step was to invite potential franchisees to a 'Discovery Day'. There, they could get an immersive experience of what running a 'Lemons by Bobby' stand would be like. This would also serve as a chance for Bobby to gauge their enthusiasm and commitment to quality—traits non-negotiable for anyone looking to become a part of the lemonade reign.

The time approached to put all these preparations to the test. The 'Lemons by Bobby' website, freshly squeezed with vibrant content and testimonials, now also featured a section for interested franchisee applicants. Bobby and Mr. Vozar crafted an application process that was thorough yet approachable, much like the brand itself. Bobby's days were now filled with a mix of schoolwork and business meetings, a balance that sometimes seemed overwhelming, but mostly exhilarating.

One snowy morning, Bobby stepped out to the lemonade stand, now functioning as his office, and took a deep, icy breath. The entrepreneurial fire within him never felt warmer. This was the culmination of months of planning, learning, and, above all, dreaming. And now it was time to see if the world was ready to share in the dream of 'Lemons by Bobby'. With the 'Discovery Day' date set, Bobby felt a fusion of nervousness and excitement. The snow outside may have blanketed the world in white, but inside the lemonade stand-turned-office, ideas and anticipation bloomed in vibrant colors. Flyers had been distributed, social media posts had been shared, and the website buzzed with activity as applications trickled in. Each applicant seemed to have caught a glimpse of Bobby's passion and wanted to be a part of it.

Mr. Vozar, becoming more of a business mentor by the day, suggested that they should also prepare a welcoming speech and a presentation that captured the ethos of 'Lemons by Bobby'. They spent several evenings perfecting their message, aiming to inspire the same entrepreneurial spirit in others that Bobby felt every day. Mr. Vozar reminded Bobby of the importance of selecting individuals who not only had the financial capacity to invest but also shared his vision and values.

The big day arrived, with fresh snow creating a picturesque setting for the inaugural 'Discovery Day'. Bobby, though visibly anxious, had an air of professionalism about him that seemed well beyond his years. As prospective franchisees arrived, they were greeted with the scent of fresh lemons and the cheerful tunes that had become synonymous with the brand's friendly image. The lemonade stand was decked out in brand colors, complete with banners and a display video showing happy customers and Bobby's journey.

After the initial meet-and-greet session, Bobby took to the stage that Mr. Vozar had proudly helped him set up in the school auditorium. The presentation went off without a hitch, showcasing the meticulous planning, potential profitability, and the heartfelt story behind 'Lemons by Bobby'. Questions were asked, answered, and as the day went on, Bobby felt increasingly confident that he was not just building a business, but a community. Mr. Vozar watched from the sidelines, a silent pride in his eyes as he witnessed his protégé shine.

As the day drew to a close, Bobby spoke to the gathered crowd, his voice steady yet imbued with the sincerity of a passionate founder. 'Together, we are not just selling lemonade; we are serving a slice of sunshine that represents togetherness, determination, and the sweetness of success,' he concluded, his gaze sweeping across the audience who erupted into an enthusiastic applause. With Mr.

Vozar's help, Bobby collected application forms, eager to review them with a careful optimism about the future.

Days passed, as Bobby, with guidance from Mr. Vozar, began the difficult task of selecting the first batch of franchise owners. They spent hours reviewing applications, conducting interviews, and discussing potential locations for the new stands. A wholesome sense of pride swelled within Bobby as he realized he was no longer just a kid with a lemonade stand; he was an entrepreneur molding the dreams of others into reality.

In the quiet moments between his increasingly rare free periods in school, Bobby poured over textbooks, his commitment to his education undiminished. 'Success in business is important, but so is your education, Bobby,' Mr. Vozar would often remind him. And as each day presented new challenges and victories, Bobby Lemons understood the delicate dance between his burgeoning empire and the pursuit of academic excellence.Bobby and Mr. Vozar sat in the back room of the original 'Lemons by Bobby' stand, their heads bent over a thick stack of applications. Each one represented a person eager to spread the sweet and tart flavors of Lemon's legacy far beyond their small town. With Mr. Vozar's business acumen and Bobby's infectious enthusiasm, they meticulously sorted through the hopefuls.

'This one seems really passionate about customer service,' said Bobby, pointing at a paragraph in one of the applications. 'And they have a great location spotted in their neighborhood.'

Mr. Vozar nodded in agreement. 'And here's another who has experience managing a small business. Remember, we're not just looking for people with resources; we're looking for individuals who embody the spirit of 'Lemons by Bobby'. They need to understand the brand.'

The brand. It was a word that still felt surreal to Bobby. He remembered the days when 'Lemons by Bobby' was just a hand-painted sign and a pitcher of homemade lemonade. Now it was a symbol, a story of community and entrepreneurship that touched the lives of many.

Hours slipped by as they debated the virtues and potential of each applicant. Some were easy to agree upon; they had the perfect combination of passion, experience, and the right intentions. Others, less clear-cut, sparked deep discussions that tested their vision for the brand's future.

Finally, after what felt like an eternity, they had their list. The first franchise owners of 'Lemons by Bobby'. The next step was to bring them together for training, to imbue them with the knowledge and values that had made Bobby's original stand a beacon of youthful success.

'These folks are going to rely on us,' Mr. Vozar said, his voice reflecting the gravity of their choices. 'We've got to do right by them, make sure they're set up for success.'

'Absolutely, we're a family now,' Bobby replied, his eyes bright. 'We're going to teach them everything we know. But first, I've got a math test to ace tomorrow!'

And with a laugh and a shake of heads at the remarkable journey ahead, they flipped off the light switch and locked up for the night, the pile of newly minted franchise contracts resting securely on the desk.

Amid the organized chaos of franchising, Bobby's days were a blur of business decisions and algebra homework, but every step felt like a milestone. 'Lemons by Bobby' was not just a stand. It was an idea – one sweet cup at a time, changing the world. The next day dawned bright and early for Bobby Lemons. Despite the additional responsibilities of his growing business, he made sure to allocate time for studying. The math test was important to him, not just as an academic requirement, but as a personal challenge. He didn't want to let Mr. Vozar down, who always encouraged him to strike a balance between entrepreneurship and education. After acing his math test, a sense of accomplishment filled Bobby's spirits as he walked to the now-familiar spot where his original lemonade stand still operated.

Mr. Vozar greeted him with a smile that could rival the sunniest of days. 'I heard about the math test, Bobby. Well done!' he exclaimed. The pride in Mr. Vozar's voice was unmistakable. They quickly shifted gears, focusing on the task at hand – the first training session for the 'Lemons by Bobby' franchise owners. The training room was set up in the community center, with posters and infographics displaying key concepts that had been key to their success. Bobby felt a flutter of nerves; these were people who believed in his brand, willing to invest their time and money into his vision.

Each franchise owner was given a personalized folder containing operational guidelines, marketing strategies, and financial management tips. Bobby stepped forward, clearing his throat. As he began to speak, his initial apprehension dissolved into a confident flow of words. He shared his journey, the obstacles he had faced, and how he overcame them with Mr. Vozar's mentorship.

The franchise owners listened intently, taking notes and asking questions. Mr. Vozar joined in, providing insights into business analytics and customer satisfaction. Their combined effort made for a comprehensive training session that left the new business owners feeling ready and motivated. As the day wound down, handshakes and smiles were exchanged, and Bobby felt a profound sense of camaraderie with his new partners.

That evening, after a long day of training, Bobby sat at his kitchen table surrounded by homework and business papers. The future locations of 'Lemons by Bobby' franchises were marked on a map, stretching like a network of lemon-scented dreams across the landscape. He allowed himself the brief satisfaction of seeing how far they'd come before turning his attention back to his algebra homework. Success in business was sweet, but Bobby knew that the knowledge he gained in school was the foundation upon which he could build an even brighter future.

The Lemonade Franchise

The gentle hum of the suburb filled the air as Bobby woke up to another gorgeous day, the sun promising the perfect weather for lemonade sales. After downing a quick breakfast and trading jokes with his supportive parents, he hopped on his bike, feeling the morning breeze rush past him as he rode towards his prized stand. Today was not just about sales; it was about growth and the promising challenge that franchising presented.

With the first wave of franchise owners trained and eager, Bobby and Mr. Vozar met up early to discuss the next steps. "You know, Bobby," Mr. Vozar started, adjusting the brim of his hat against the morning sun, "franchising isn't just about replicating a business model. It's about maintaining the quality and the essence of what made 'Lemons by Bobby' a neighborhood hit."

Bobby nodded, understanding the importance of consistency. As they talked, they reviewed potential sites for the new franchises, discussed long-term supply deals with local farmers, and brainstormed marketing strategies that would encompass the individuality of each new stand while staying true to the brand.

As the days grew longer and the first franchise locations began to take shape, Bobby found himself dividing his time ever more. Mornings were dedicated to tutoring sessions for his upcoming school projects, his afternoons were swallowed by the nitty-gritty of business expansion, and evenings were for visiting each upcoming franchise location, ensuring the owners felt supported.

He learned the tools of the trade in balancing the numerous hats he had to wear. Nevertheless, the passion he had for both his academic and entrepreneurial pursuits fueled him, making the exhausting days worthwhile. Bobby's efforts seemed to be paying off; every time he checked in with a franchise owner, he was greeted with enthusiasm and positive updates.

One late afternoon, as Bobby reviewed inventory lists and sales forecasts, Mr. Vozar approached him with a set of freshly printed 'Lemons by Bobby' banners. "It's vital to create excitement around the grand openings," Mr. Vozar explained, holding up the vibrant yellow material that fluttered in the breeze. Bobby smiled, thinking how his small lemonade stand was about to make a big splash in the community.

In the weeks that followed, 'Lemons by Bobby' became more than a stand—it became a local phenomenon. Each new franchise brought its own unique flair, yet followed the golden standard that Bobby had established. From the original roadside stand to the inviting franchises scattered throughout the town, the tale of Bobby Lemons and his refreshing venture rippled far and wide.Bobby's days were filled with a flurry of activities as the schedule for the grand openings loomed over the horizon. In the mornings, he would diligently attend his classes, jotting down notes with one hand and sketching out promotional designs with the other. After school, he'd cycle to each new 'Lemons by Bobby' location to guide the franchisees in the art of mixing the perfect blend of tangy and sweet lemonade.

In between, Bobby and Mr. Vozar met with local suppliers to negotiate deals for lemons, sugar, and other essentials, ensuring each franchise would offer the same delicious taste customers had come to expect. Bobby learned to manage his time and energy effectively, grabbing small moments of rest while skimming through his economics textbook or tuning into business podcasts.

Marketing strategies became the talk of the town as Bobby, with Mr. Vozar's guidance, harnessed the power of social media to fuel anticipation. They crafted posts showcasing the magic behind the lemonade-making process and shared stories of satisfied customers that earned hundreds of likes and shares. As comments poured in, Bobby interacted with his growing fan base, creating an authentic connection that other brands could only envy.

The evening before the grand openings, Bobby visited each location, inspecting every detail from the cleanliness of the counters to the position of signage. He wanted to ensure that customers would not only enjoy the best lemonade but also an experience that touched their hearts. He spent hours with franchisees, rehearsing the ribbon-cutting ceremony, and sharing the contagious enthusiasm that this expansion deserved.

Everything was falling into place, and Bobby couldn't help but feel a surge of pride. The once simple, wooden lemonade stand he started on a whim was now a household name. And tomorrow, it would spread even further. Sleep was elusive that night as Bobby lay in bed, envisioning the ribbon-cutting scenes and the smiling faces that would accompany them.At the crack of dawn, Bobby was already on his feet, the butterflies in his stomach doing somersaults. This was the day he had been dreaming of for weeks, the day 'Lemons by Bobby' would make its grand debut in neighborhoods across the city. He donned his signature lemon-patterned tie, which had become somewhat of a lucky charm, and set out to visit each of the new locations.

The first rays of sunlight were painting the sky in hues of orange and pink as Bobby arrived at the inaugural franchise spot. The smell of fresh lemons wafted through the air, merging with the scent of newly printed banners and clean, wooden counters. The franchise owners, a young couple brimming with excitement, welcomed Bobby with open arms. Together, they did a final check of the supplies – cups, straws, napkins, and, of course, the lemons, freshly picked from the groves.

As people began to trickle in, drawn by the buzz on social media and the vibrant balloons dancing in the early morning breeze, Bobby could see the fruits of his labor coming to life. The couple cut the ribbon amidst cheers, and the first pitcher of lemonade was poured. Camera flashes captured the moment, sure to be shared and reshared on every local news feed.

Noon brought with it a scorching sun and a thirsty crowd. Lines snaked around corners as locals and tourists alike clamored for a glass of the famous lemonade. At each franchised lemonade stand Bobby visited, he was greeted by similar scenes – lines of customers, the clinking of ice, and the collective satisfaction of ice-cold refreshment on a hot summer day.

To Bobby's surprise, even Mr. Vozar stopped by, his proud smile telling more than words could. 'I knew you had it in you, Bobby,' he said, clapping him on the back. 'You've not just learned the ropes; you've skipped them.'

The hours flew by in a blur of yellow and laughter. As the sun began to dip below the horizon, Bobby gathered his franchisees for a celebratory dinner. Over glasses of lemonade, of course, they shared stories of the day's successes and the occasional mishap that only added flavor to the experience. The day was wrapping up, but for 'Lemons by Bobby', it was just the beginning of a sweet, nationwide adventure.The evening unfolded like the peels of a ripe lemon — full of zest and surprise. Under twinkling lights, the franchisees gathered, buzzing with the electricity of shared triumph and dreams achieved. Plates clinked and glasses chimed in toasts, the latter filled with the hallmark beverage that united them all. Bobby, ever the gracious host, stood and raised his glass high. 'To all of you, who have taken this journey with me, I say thank you. Today is a testament to what we can achieve together.' The table erupted into applause, a harmonious soundtrack to a day they'd never forget.

As the night wore on, the initial euphoria gave way to more serious discussions. Dreams were great, but as Mr. Vozar often said, 'A dream without a plan is just a wish.' And Bobby Lemons was not in the business of making wishes. 'We need to strategize,' Bobby said, once the clapping subsided and all eyes were on him. 'It's imperative that as we grow, we maintain the quality that got us here. Standardization across all locations is key. But I want to hear from you. What challenges are you facing? And how can we, as a collective, address them?' The franchisees shared concerns — supply chain consistency, staffing, local competition — and Bobby listened, nodding, his mind already whirring with solutions.

After much deliberation, they established a 'Best Practices' protocol, complete with regular check-ins and an annual franchisee conference to exchange knowledge and innovations. Bobby saw the spark in their eyes, the same one he'd had when he first pitched a lemon to his neighborhood — the spark of passion that turns the mundane into the extraordinary.

As the conversation turned to future expansion, Mr. Vozar, who'd been listening intently, leaned forward. 'Remember, Bobby, with each new branch, your brand's story is told anew. Make sure it's always a story of quality, community, and the unwavering spirit of entrepreneurship.' Bobby nodded, his respect for his mentor deepening. 'I won't forget that, Mr. Vozar. You've taught me that a business's heart lies in its story. That's something we'll carry with every glass we serve.'

They left the dinner energized, their minds fertile soil for the seeds of expansion sown that night. Bobby couldn't help feeling like he'd squeezed every drop of success from the day, but he knew the real work was just beginning. It was one thing to open franchises; it was another to foster them.As the last bites of the decadent dessert were enjoyed, the atmosphere was light yet filled with determination. The camaraderie among franchisees at the dinner table was genuine

-- a collective group of individuals united by a vision crafted by a young boy and his lemonade stand.

Bobby had spent the majority of the evening absorbing wisdom and advice like a sponge, but now it was his turn to speak.

'I want to thank each and every one of you for believing in this,' Bobby began, his voice steady and full of gratitude. 'We're not just selling lemonade; we're sharing a piece of happiness, a sip of sunshine with our community. I'm committed to ensuring we all thrive, but that means we need to keep learning, adapting, and growing together.'

After the dinner, back in the quiet of his room, Bobby's mind raced with the magnitude of what they had discussed. His notebook was open to a page filled with bullet points, tasks, and ideas. 'Franchise Training Program,' one heading read, followed by 'Quality Control Measures,' and 'Marketing Strategies.' He knew these weren't just ideas; they would soon have to be concrete plans in action.

Over the next few weeks, Bobby and his core team worked tirelessly. They mapped out a comprehensive training program for new franchisees, ensuring that the same level of care and passion that went into the original lemonade recipe was maintained everywhere. Secret shopper programs were rolled out to maintain a high standard of service, and Bobby even started a monthly newsletter titled 'The Lemonade Chronicle' to keep everyone in the loop.

But success always breeds new challenges. Competition began to notice the buzz around Bobby's burgeoning franchise. Some tried to mimic the flavors, the branding, and even the story. Bobby, however, remained undeterred. He knew that authenticity couldn't be replicated, and he doubled down on community engagement. He sponsored local sports teams, held lemonade-making contests, and awarded scholarships to young entrepreneurs.

It wasn't long before the local news wanted to cover 'Bobby Lemons, the young entrepreneur who turned his summer project into a sensational franchise.' His story was both humbling and inspiring, a narrative that resonated with all who heard it.Bobby's lemonade was now more than just a thirst-quencher; it had become a community symbol for ambition and youthful entrepreneurship. Parents brought their children, hopeful that some of Bobby's diligence and creativity would rub off on them. Teenagers gathered at the stand, talking and sipping on the now-famous 'Lemon Lightning' blend.

In the midst of all this, Mr. Vozar guided Bobby through the nuances of franchising his business model. 'You've proven that your lemonade and customer service are top-notch, Bobby,' Mr. Vozar began, 'but franchising will require you to create a system that can be replicated while also maintaining that high standard.'

Bobby learned about the importance of a franchise disclosure document, a detailed outline for prospective franchisees about what to expect and what is expected of them. Mr. Vozar talked about royalty fees, branding guidelines, and the importance of selecting the right partners who shared Bobby's vision and commitment.

The local newspaper's feature on 'Bobby Lemons' hit the stands, and suddenly, Bobby was fielding calls from interested investors, curious customers, and even some national news outlets. The attention was exhilarating but also overwhelming. 'Just remember to keep your roots in mind,' Mr. Vozar reminded Bobby. 'Your brand is about quality and community - never let go of that.'

Bobby started his day even earlier than usual now, ensuring he could oversee operations, connect with his staff, and respond to the tidal wave of inquiries. He recruited a small but dedicated PR team to manage the media attention and maintain the stand's heartfelt persona.

One sunny Tuesday, Bobby received a call that would set the course for the next phase of his venture. A prominent business mogul had caught wind of Bobby's story and was interested in backing his franchise expansion - but with conditions that could change Bobby's original vision.

For Bobby, the decision loomed large over his future. He pondered whether this investment was a leap in the right direction or a step away from what made his lemonade stand special in the first place. He turned to Mr. Vozar, who simply said, 'Bobby, whatever you choose, make sure it's a decision that you can live with at the end of every day.'

As the sun dipped below the horizon, casting a golden glow over his lemonade stand, Bobby realized that this was just the beginning. He was not just selling lemonade; he was crafting a legacy.Bobby's thoughts swirled with the myriad possibilities that this new investment could bring. The business mogul, Mr. Kingston, had given him a glossy brochure illustrating high-tech lemonade stands, comprehensive training programs for franchisees, and a marketing campaign that could put Bobby's Lemonade on billboards across the state. The numbers were convincing, the potential for growth immense, but Bobby's gut held a kernel of doubt. His business, his creation, could become unrecognizable.

He turned to Mr. Vozar once more, 'How do I know if I'm making the right choice?' Mr. Vozar took off his glasses, cleaning them thoughtfully before looking Bobby in the eye. 'You've learned the business, now it's time to understand your values. Will you measure success in revenue, or the smiles of kids on a hot summer day? There's no right answer, only your answer, Bobby.'

Bobby took a long walk that evening, past the parks where he first dreamt of his lemonade stand, past the school where he had pitched his idea to a curious Mr. Vozar. He stopped, finally, under the old oak tree where he had first set up shop. The choice was clear. He called Mr. Kingston the next morning. 'I'm grateful for your offer,' Bobby began, 'But I can't lose the heart of my business—the community touch, the homemade recipe, the hand-drawn signs. Maybe we can find a middle ground?'

Mr. Kingston was silent on the other end for a moment but then his voice picked up, warm and amiable. 'Bobby, I've invested in many businesses, but none had an owner who knew their soul as well as you know yours. Let's talk about that middle ground.'

So talks began, with Bobby holding firm to his vision while embracing the wisdom he had garnered from Mr. Vozar and his own experience. The next week was filled with discussions, phone calls, and negotiations. As the final details were ironed out, Bobby felt a swell of pride. He was about to take his humble lemonade stand to new heights, all while keeping its spirit intact.

A Lemon-Scented Future

Bobby poured over spreadsheets and business plans, each figure a testament to the transformation his small stand had undergone. With every sip sold, his smile had widened, and with every satisfied customer, the reputation of Bobby's Lemonade had sweetened in his local community.

Mr. Kingston, with his sharp suits and sharper business acumen, was a stark contrast to the laid-back corner where Bobby's stand proudly displayed its hand-painted sign. Yet, it was the mogul's keen eye that saw the kernel of potential in Bobby's earnest endeavor. Now, they sat opposite each other, a wooden table between them cluttered with contracts and proposals.

'It's settled then,' Mr. Kingston said, offering a pen to Bobby. 'We franchise, but your ethos becomes a blueprint, a core ingredient that can't be altered or omitted. It's what makes Bobby's Lemonade special.'

Bobby took the pen, his hand steady. 'And every franchise owner will spend a day at the original stand, learning the ropes from me.' He was insistent on preserving the charm and quality of his beloved stand, and Mr. Kingston had agreed. Bobby would cultivate a training program that would imbibe his values into each franchisee.

'That's the spirit, kid,' Mr. Kingston replied with a nod. 'I like your style. It's more than just business; it's about community.'

As Bobby signed, a myriad of feelings cascaded through him – excitement, nervousness, triumph. He was venturing into uncharted territory, but he wasn't alone. Mr. Vozar's lessons echoed in his mind, a grounding presence amid the whirlwind of success.

In the days that followed, Bobby worked tirelessly to uphold his promise. The original lemonade stand underwent a careful makeover, ready to serve not just lemonade, but lessons in service, quality, and community. Local schools began field trips to the stand, where Bobby shared his story and taught the basics of entrepreneurship. The heart of Bobby's Lemonade was beating stronger than ever.

Bobby would sometimes pause and look back at the journey so far. From the first day he pitched his stand, selling only two glasses, to the bustling hotspot it had become, he knew Mr. Vozar's wisdom had been instrumental. Cost of Goods Sold (COGS) was now a term as familiar to him as the recipe for his lemonade; revenue and expenses danced around in his head as he made decisions. He understood the importance of gross profit, calculating net profit with ease, and most importantly, the power of marketing and community engagement. 'For a truly successful business, you must know your numbers as well as you know your customers,' Mr. Vozar would say.

As evening approached, the stand remained a beacon of the neighborhood, its lights casting a warm glow on passersby. Bobby's dream had scaled up from its simple roots to branches that extended towards the future. The lemonade was still the same refreshing concoction, but the boy who made it had transformed entirely.

Now, customers didn't just come for a drink; they came for the experience Bobby had created—an experience that Bobby was soon to replicate across the country.It was as if every drop of lemonade served also poured a story for the customers. The tale of a young entrepreneur's resilience and the birth of a business out of pure determination and learned expertise. Bobby often found himself lost in thought, reflecting on the swarm of lessons that had been imparted by his mentor, Mr. Vozar. Concepts like 'economies of scale' and 'customer lifetime value' were no longer just phrases but integral aspects of decision-making for the evolving franchise.

Bobby recognized the need to establish a strong foundation for his franchise model. He sought out vibrant, community-centric locations for his new stands. The scouting trips were exhaustive yet thrilling. Each potential site was evaluated not just on foot traffic but also on the community's ethos—a key ingredient that made his original stand so beloved. As he ventured from his home turf, the stories of people and neighborhoods painted a promising canvas for the expansion of Bobby's Lemonade.

Franchisee selection became his next hurdle. Bobby knew the soul of his business lay in its people. He organized open days at his original stand, inviting interested parties to experience a day-in-the-life of a Bobby's Lemonade stand. Through these sessions, he encountered a diverse array of enthusiasts, from retired veterans looking for a fresh start to young college graduates brimming with entrepreneurial spirit. Bobby interviewed them with a focus on their passion for quality and their dedication to fostering community, two of the pillars that Mr. Vozar had emphasized in business success.

Maintaining the quality of the lemonade was paramount. Bobby spent weeks refining the operation manuals, ensuring that every detail from lemon zest to sugar ratios was meticulously documented. Training programs were established, where franchisees were immersed in the craft of lemonade making under Bobby's watchful eye. He took particular pride in educating them on customer relations, passing on Mr. Vozar's tenet that 'each customer interaction is a seed planted for future growth'.

However, the challenges of consistency loomed large as Bobby pondered the complexities of supply chains and staff training across multiple locations. The idea of his lemonade losing its soul in a bid for expansion haunted him. Determined to preserve the 'Bobbyness' of each cup served, he devised a rigorous quality control system, and decided to use only the vendors that could guarantee the freshness and quality of ingredients worthy of the Bobby's Lemonade name.

Amidst the whirlwind of activities, Bobby's phone echoed with the ringtone he had assigned for Mr. Vozar. His heart hummed with anticipation and gratitude as he answered, knowing that his mentor's voice would carry the wisdom to guide him through this expansion phase. 'Remember, Bobby, it's not just about how many stands you open; it's about how many lives you touch with each one,' Mr. Vozar's voice rekindled the flame of Bobby's mission. The call ended with Bobby scribbling down yet another pearl of wisdom from Mr. Vozar, a reminder that the journey of entrepreneurship was perpetual learning. The days that followed were a kaleidoscope of challenges and triumphs. Bobby traveled from one potential franchise location to another, greeted by eager faces and buzzing communities excited to welcome the refreshing zest of Bobby's Lemonade. His eyes would scan each site, envisioning families and friends gathering around, laughter spilling over the clinking of ice cubes in the glasses of his signature lemonade.

Choosing the right franchisees proved to be as crucial as the locations themselves. Bobby sought individuals who shared his values and enthusiasm for quality and community engagement. He didn't just want business partners; he wanted ambassadors of the brand he had lovingly built. Franchisee training sessions became regular occurrences, where Bobby conveyed not just the recipes for the drinks, but the essence of customer service and community that was the heart of Bobby's Lemonade.

Meanwhile, Bobby worked tirelessly with a local designer to create operation manuals that were not only informative but also engaging. He knew that the success of each franchise hinged on the understanding and execution of these guidelines. Quality control systems were tested and tweaked, ensuring that the lemonade that made his stand a local hit would remain consistent in every new outlet.

The first few franchise locations opened to much fanfare, but not without hiccups. Bobby was soon handling supplier issues, where one franchise received a batch of lemons that weren't up to his standards. Rather than seeing it as a setback, Bobby treated it as an opportunity to reinforce the importance of quality with his suppliers and franchisees. Another time, a miscommunication with a contractor almost led to a grand opening delay. Bobby, channeling Mr. Vozar's teachings, kept his cool and worked out a solution that kept everyone happy and on schedule.

Word of mouth spread like wildfire, and Bobby's Lemonade began to receive media attention. Local bloggers, food critics, and even a regional news station featured stories about the stand that was making a sweet splash in the community. Bobby ensured that the narrative remained focused on the business's roots, often inviting Mr. Vozar to these interviews to share insights on the educational aspect of the enterprise.

As the sun set on another bustling day, Bobby stood outside his original lemonade stand, now surrounded by a handful of thriving franchises. He sipped on his classic recipe, a blend that tasted of hard work and sunny days. He knew there was more to learn, more strategies to refine, and more lives to touch. But in this moment, he revelled in the sweet success and the knowledge that his journey had inspired and quenched the thirst of a community.As he reflected on the unfolding success story of Bobby's Lemonade, Bobby Lemons couldn't help but smile at the irony of his initial struggles. The lessons he received from Mr. Vozar - his once schoolteacher, now business mentor - resonated deeply within him. Bobby learned the fundamentals of COGS, revenue, gross profit, and net profit, but he also understood the profound impact of maintaining a positive brand image and community engagement. With each new franchise, Bobby insisted on a hands-on approach to training, ensuring everyone understood the core values that made the first lemonade stand a beacon of entrepreneurial spirit.

But with expansion came new hurdles. A vendor delivered a batch of lemons that were far below the quality standards Bobby had set. To address this, Bobby had to negotiate and enforce stricter quality checks with suppliers, underscoring that no compromise would be made on the signature taste of Bobby's Lemonade. In a similar vein, a misinterpretation of design specs by a contractor led to a delay in opening a new location. Bobby took it in his stride, leveraging the opportunity to tighten up communication protocols and project management guidelines for future builds.

Media attention continued to pour in, with local bloggers and food critics eager to share the vibrant story of Bobby's Lemonade.

Bobby understood that publicity could be a double-edged sword and was careful to curate the message, always bringing it back to the quality of the product and the educational values it stood for. Mr. Vozar, through these media appearances, became something of a local celebrity himself, eloquently tying the concepts of business education with real-world success.

One afternoon, as Bobby scrutinized sales data and trend charts, he couldn't shake off a sense of discomfort. The figures were promising, yet they seemed impersonal. It struck him that amidst the spreadsheets and financial meetings, he needed to ensure the soul of Bobby's Lemonade wasn't drowned out by numbers. He decided to schedule regular visits to each franchise, not to audit, but to interact - to tell stories, listen to customers, and remind his team why they squeezed every lemon with care. It was this blend of corporate diligence and heartfelt connection that kept the magic alive.

As he continued to balance spreadsheets with smiles, Bobby knew this was just the beginning. His vision for Bobby's Lemonade was grander than what the eye could see – a place where communities could come together, where life's lessons were as plentiful as the lemon slices in the pitchers, and where each glass served was a toast to possibility and growth. Bobby smiled, fixing his gaze on the horizon - where the next dawn would bring new challenges, new opportunities, and a zest for success that no obstacle could sour.Morning dew still clung to the world as Bobby unlocked the door to his original lemonade stand. It might now be the flagship for a burgeoning franchise, but to Bobby, it would always be where it all started — a small piece of wood and hope on the sidewalk. Today was different, though; today, this little stand was host to a celebration of success, community, and learning.

Streamers winked in the gentle embrace of the early breeze, and fresh lemons, the size of baseballs, awaited their destiny alongside crystal-clear pitchers. Bobby had insisted on a celebration to thank his loyal customers, and in a stroke of brilliant simplicity, he decided to call it 'Lemonade Appreciation Day'. A banner, celebrating the event, stretched above the stand, as the sun peeked just enough to bestow its golden approval.

Mr. Vozar was there too, of course. With a clipboard in hand, he observed the setup keenly, always the teacher. 'Remember, Bobby, even celebrations need to be well-planned. It's not just a party; it's a customer experience event,' he'd told Bobby earlier. Those words were taken to heart, and Bobby planned activities and giveaways that were not just fun but authentically reflected the core values of his brand.

As the day progressed, faces, both familiar and novel, came to share in the joy of Bobby's journey. They marveled at the stand transformed by success, raising their glasses to cheer for the young entrepreneur whose vision and tenacity had become manifest in the vibrant stalls before them.

Nearby, a local newspaper reporter tapped notes into her smartphone, already outlining the feature she'd write on Bobby's rising star as a business icon in the community. Her eyes followed Bobby as he mingled, laughed, and sometimes leaned in to share the secrets of his success with the curious and the aspiring.

It was in these moments, his sleeves rolled up as he helped a new franchise owner perfect the blend of their lemonade 'to that special Bobby's standard', that the lessons from Mr. Vozar crystalized into something more profound than mere business practice. They were life lessons, principles to be applied far beyond the confines of his refreshing empire.

As the sun dipped low, signaling an end to 'Lemonade Appreciation Day', Bobby stood before his first lemonade stand, now dormant in the crescendo of evening chatter. His heart was full, his mind raced with ideas, and his eyes sparkled with the reflection of a day well-spent. It wasn't just about the lemonade anymore — it was about the connections, the smiles, the community coming together. Bobby knew, this was what success tasted like.

Hearing the soft clear of a throat, he turned to find Mr. Vozar beside him, wearing a small, proud smile, 'You've done well, Bobby. Remember, though, this is just a milestone. The learning never stops.' With those words, night settled, and the future seemed as bright as ever. As customers dwindled and the lights dimmed, Bobby etched every moment into his memory — a sweet reminder of how far he'd come and the endless possibilities that lay ahead. As the evening air cooled and the bustle of 'Lemonade Appreciation Day' subsided, Bobby Lemons stood amidst the few lingering patrons, absorbing the laughter and chit-chat that animated his flagship stand. The aroma of fresh citrus lingered amidst the twinkling lights that framed his little empire. He glanced at the framed dollar bill on the wall, the first he ever earned, and felt a wave of nostalgia combined with immense pride.

Bobby's thoughts were interrupted by the enthusiastic praises of a local reporter who had vigorously taken notes throughout the event. 'Bobby, your story is inspirational,' she said with a beaming smile. 'A teenager turning a lemonade stand into a thriving business is something our readers will love. I can see the headline now: "The Sweet Success of Bobby's Lemon Blitz!"' Bobby's cheeks flushed with a modest pride as he thanked her, cognizant of the fact that his endeavors were gaining recognition beyond his wildest dreams.

Mr. Vozar watched from a distance, his teacher's eye observing not just the student he'd mentored, but the young entrepreneur who had taken those lessons to heart. 'All that you've learned, you must pass it on,' Mr. Vozar advised as they began stacking chairs together. 'You have the power to not just run a business but also to inspire and teach others.' Bobby nodded, knowing that part of his future plans would be to mentor young entrepreneurs, sharing the valuable lessons he had learned.

Later, as he locked the front door of the stand, the plans for the next day began taking form in his mind. He was scheduled to visit his other franchise locations, checking in on operations and ensuring the quality and service that had become synonymous with the name 'Bobby's Lemon Blitz'. It was crucial to Bobby that every cup of lemonade served was as good as the one from his original stand.

Bobby also committed to spending time each week on research and development. 'Lemonade was just the beginning,' he mused. New ideas, from seasonal flavors to possible partnerships with local farmers for fresh produce, swirled in his head. He was dedicated to innovation but was equally determined to uphold the core values Mr. Vozar had taught him: integrity, community, and passion.

As night embraced his little corner of the world, Bobby locked up and turned to take one last look at his flagship stand, a beacon in the quiet evening. He took a deep breath, the scents of his success mingling with the responsibilities that lay ahead. His journey was far from over, it was evolving, with new challenges and opportunities on the horizon.Bobby strolled home, the cool night air making him wrap his jacket tighter around him. His mind raced faster than his steps, with visions of lemonade cups filling every city corner. Mr. Vozar's business lessons echoed in his heart, each step resonating with a commitment to take his lemonade stand to new heights.

The following morning, after a night of restless scheming, Bobby set out to visit each of his franchise locations. He stepped into the first one with the eye of an eagle, noting the vibrant colors of the stand, the neatness of the serving area, and the enthusiastic smiles of his employees. His presence was warmly received, his advice respectfully considered, and his encouragement readily accepted. 'It's all about the customer experience,' he reminded them, recounting Mr. Vozar's words on the importance of customer satisfaction.

In each visit, Bobby left behind a nugget of wisdom, a strategy session, and an employee pep talk that had his teams buzzing with renewed vigor. By his fourth visit, the word had spread: Bobby Lemons was not just an owner; he was a leader who worked alongside his employees, ensuring every glass of lemonade was worthy of the franchise's name.

Yet, there was more work to be done. After ensuring his current operations were smooth, Bobby dedicated time for innovation. He sketched out new contraptions that could zest lemons quicker, stirred experimental flavors in his kitchen, and even tested biodegradable cups. He often burned the midnight oil, his passion for improvement only matched by his newfound acumen for business.

Amidst this whirlwind of activity, Bobby knew he needed to scale his ambitions. Indeed, he was already in talks with a neighboring cafe for a collaborative summer special. 'Possibilities are like lemons,' he thought with a chuckle, 'there seems to always be more to squeeze out.'

As the sun set on yet another productive day, Bobby sat down at his desk, exhausted but exhilarated. He pulled out a piece of paper and began to draft his vision for the future of his franchise.Bobby drew a deep breath, the scent of fresh lemons lingering in his office. The office was modest, a reflection of his humble beginnings, but it was filled with the enthusiasm and dreams of a burgeoning entrepreneur. He'd come a long way from the shaky start of merely a wooden stand and hand-painted sign. Vivid memories of that first tepid summer breeze, accompanied by the jingle of loose change in his pocket, remained etched in his heart. But it was not a time for nostalgia; it was time to envision the future.

Leaning over his desk, Bobby began to sketch the framework of his grand vision. 'Efficiency,' he wrote in bold letters, 'the cog that turns the wheel.' Below it, he scribbled notes on streamlining production processes and optimizing inventory management. He envisioned a standardized training system that would ensure consistency in customer service across all locations. To his mind, these were the arteries that would feed the lifeblood of his enterprise. With each idea, his pencil moved faster, as if trying to keep pace with the racing thoughts in his head.

Bobby knew that expansion also meant a greater societal impact. He wanted his business to be an integral part of the community—a place that symbolized not just refreshment, but rejuvenation for the spirit. This, he believed, could be furthered through collaboration. As such, he made a mental note to finalize the details with the neighboring cafe, envisioning a fusion of flavors that could captivate the palates of their shared clientele.

Hours passed as light faded and gave way to the crisp glow of his desk lamp. Before him lay the blueprint of a future potent with promise. One by one, he began checking off completed sections, his excitement palpable with each tick of affirmation. 'Mr. Vozar would be proud,' he thought. The teacher's lessons had become the foundation of a flourishing business model. From grasping the critical nature of COGS to the innovative maneuvers in marketing, Bobby had internalized each lesson, turning them into stepping stones towards success.

He culminated his vision in a comprehensive strategy document, a roadmap towards the unwritten chapters of his venture. This document would soon circulate among his growing network of franchises, a testament to the collective efforts and insights drawn from customers, employees, and mentors alike.

As midnight approached, Bobby finally set down his pencil. The office was silent, save for the soft hum of ambition lingering in the air. He stretched, his body weary but his spirit unyielding. Tomorrow, he would begin the task of breathing life into his plans, imbuing each franchise with the fresh zest of his vision.

With his goals crystallized on paper, Bobby headed home, the night whispering promises of lemon-infused tomorrows. 'Tomorrow,' he affirmed, 'we build the future.'

Juicing the Competition

The next morning, Bobby awoke with the chirping of birds and the gentle caress of the early sun on his face. Excited for the challenges ahead, he sprang from his bed, dressed quickly, and biked to the closest lemonade stand in his franchise. The morning air filled his lungs, invigorating him with the feeling that today marked the beginning of a new chapter.

His employees greeted him with a mix of anticipation and curiosity as he arrived with a binder thick with new guidelines, strategies, and inspiration. He held a meeting right there on the sidewalk, detailing the operational changes, emphasizing the importance of customer service, and instilling a sense of pride in the brand. 'We're not just selling lemonade,' he told them, 'we're serving refreshment and joy!' His enthusiasm was infectious, and soon the team was buzzing with renewed energy and a desire to excel.

Bobby's resolve was tested sooner than expected. Across the street, a new stand had appeared, decked out with colorful banners and offering a variety of exotic flavors. Its owner, a savvy kid with a smile as sweet as the lemonade he peddled, was drawing in Bobby's regulars with a special grand opening offer. Bobby watched, initially unnerved, but then reminded himself of the lessons Mr. Vozar had taught him.

He pulled his team together for a quick brainstorming session, and together they rolled out a loyalty program on the spot. Customers who stayed with 'Bobby's Lemonade' would receive every fifth cup free, in addition to being entered into a monthly raffle for a free gallon of their famous drink. The move was bold and decisive, showcasing a leadership that belied Bobby's young years.

By the end of the day, as they were about to close up shop, a thrill ran through the team as one of their regulars came back across the street, drawn by the loyalty program. 'I had to give the new flavor a try, but nothing beats your classic lemonade, Bobby,' he declared, his words lifting spirits and sales alike.

It wasn't long before the word spread, and business picked up again. Bobby's early lessons in marketing and customer retention were paying off. As their competitor tried to keep up, Bobby had already initiated the next phase of his plan.

The collaboration with the neighboring cafe was next. Bobby and the cafe owner, Mrs. Cabrera, had worked out an arrangement that benefited both parties: Bobby's franchises would supply the cafe with fresh lemonade, and in exchange, the cafe would promote the stands. As they shook hands, sealing the deal, Mrs. Cabrera said with a knowing smile, 'You've got quite the head for business, Bobby. I'm glad to be on your team.'

With strategies in place and operations running smoothly, 'Bobby's Lemonade' was not just a franchise; it was becoming a community staple. Over the upcoming weeks, Bobby's stands continued to see growth. His passion for business and his innovative strategies had borne fruit far sweeter than he had ever imagined, and there was a tangible buzz in the air that something special was happening in their small town - all thanks to Bobby's unwavering vision and hard work.The loyalty program was a masterstroke. With every sip of lemonade, customers were inching closer to a free cup, and the promise of that reward kept them coming back. Bobby noticed the familiar faces, now turning into regulars, their punch cards proudly presented with each visit. The neighboring cafe's patrons could be seen with cold lemonades in hand, the fruits of Bobby's collaboration, while the cafe enjoyed the influx of customers stopping by for a pastry after their refreshing drink.

As the summer heat reached its zenith, Bobby's lemonade franchise was the oasis people sought. But the scorching sun brought competition as well. Other kids had set up stands throughout the town, their banners fluttering like challenge flags. They offered exotic flavors - mango lemonade, raspberry spritz, and even a spicy jalapeño concoction. Bobby walked by these stands with a curious eye; he sampled their offerings, complimented their efforts, and observed their operations. He realized that competition was inevitable, but it was also a chance to learn and innovate.

Mr. Vozar, his mentor and guide through the whirlwind of entrepreneurship, had taught him to respect competition and to use it as a motivator. One particular Saturday, while visiting a competing stand, he overheard a couple of kids discussing how 'Bobby's Lemonade' was just too popular to beat. 'He's got the best spot, the best taste, and even that loyalty thing we can't match!' one kid said with a mix of frustration and admiration. Bobby smiled to himself and returned to his own stand, motivated by the challenge to improve even further.

Fueled by the competitive spirit, Bobby began testing new flavors and combo offerings, creating a 'Mix of the Month' that brought an exciting twist to the classic lemonade. He also invested in eye-catching stand designs and friendly service training for his staff, ensuring that every interaction at his franchise was pleasant and memorable. The efforts paid off — sales continued to soar, and 'Bobby's Lemonade' remained a step ahead in the lemonade game.

Behind the scenes, Bobby worked tirelessly on his grand vision for the community event. He wanted it to be a day of celebration, not just for his franchise, but for the entire town. Plans were laid out for a lemonade competition, local food vendors, games for kids, and live music. 'Bobby's Big Lemon Bash' would be a day for families, friends, and neighbors to come together under the summer sun and enjoy the camaraderie and refreshment provided by their collective efforts. Bobby sent out invitations, hung posters, and even got the local radio station to announce the event. As the days counted down, anticipation built within the town.

The morning of 'Bobby's Big Lemon Bash' broke with clear blue skies and a gentle breeze that seemed to carry with it the laughter and chatter of an excited community. Bobby stood before his team, his heart swelling with pride. 'Today,' he announced, 'we celebrate not just our success, but the spirit of our town. Let's make this a day to remember!' His team cheered, ready to serve up the happiness, one cup of lemonade at a time.Early arrivals meandered about, basking in the carnival-like atmosphere that now infused the town square. Streamers dangled from the tents adorned with vibrant lemons, and the gleeful tunes of a local band wafted through the air. Children laughed as they darted around the lemon-themed games, and the scent of fresh lemonade married with the sizzle of food from pop-up stalls.

Competitors' stands, each flaunting their own twist on the classic beverage, lined the perimeter. Yet none appeared as bustling as 'Bobby's Lemonade' central booth. Bobby, now a beacon of entrepreneurial spirit in his bright yellow apron, knew that his consistent quality, customer service, and unique recipes were his standout selling points.

Still, he took no chances. Circulating through the crowd, Bobby greeted townsfolk with the graciousness of a seasoned businessman. He collected feedback, suggestions, and even noted the delighted expressions of patrons sipping his signature 'Zesty Sunshine Blend'.

But it wasn't just his lemonade that enthralled the masses. Alongside the refreshing drinks, he had set up an 'Entrepreneur's Corner', where he and Mr. Vozar offered advice to aspiring young business owners - giving back to the community that had helped him soar. This practical, yet heartwarming attraction garnered attention, emphasizing his commitment to shared growth, which differentiated him further from the competition.

As the sun reached its zenith, Bobby unveiled his pièce de résistance: a giant inflatable lemon that children could enter and learn about lemonade-making through an interactive experience. It was both educational and whimsical, hitting right at the heart of Bobby's message - merging fun with the entrepreneurial spirit. The inflatable lemon wasn't just a hit with the kids; parents were equally enchanted, sharing their enjoyment across social media, effectively amplifying the buzz for 'Bobby's Lemonade'.

The hours slipped away, filled with laughter, toasts, and the clinking of ice cubes in countless cups. Bobby's Big Lemon Bash was shaping up to be the success he envisioned.As the sun dipped lower in the sky, casting a golden hue over 'Bobby's Big Lemon Bash,' the air was vibrant with the sound of a local band playing upbeat tunes. The tables were dotted with yellow and white checkered tablecloths, and every so often, a cheer erupted from the lemon pie-eating contest, where sticky faces giggled in delight. Amongst the festivities, Bobby navigated the crowds, tablet in hand, taking note of popular flavors and ideas for new lemonade blends.

Bobby's encounter with a young brother-sister duo operating their own small lemonade stand drew a crowd. Adorable in their earnestness, they exuded a raw entrepreneurial spirit that reminded Bobby himself of why he started. Rather than see them as mere competition, he applauded their effort, bought a cup of their tangy concoction, and gave them pointers on customer engagement and presentation. Indeed, competition was stiffening, but Bobby's experience and dedication kept his business unparalleled in quality and innovation.

As the event drew to a close, Bobby orchestrated a lemonade toast. Everyone gathered, raising their glasses in unison, reveling in the sweet taste of community and success. His parents beamed at him, pride obvious in their eyes. Bobby had not only created a thriving business but had sparked a sense of entrepreneurship within the community. Looking around at the satisfied faces, it was clear that 'Bobby's Lemonade' was more than just a drink; it had become a gathering point, a source of inspiration, and a sweet slice of hometown pride.

'Bobby's Big Lemon Bash' culminated with a raffle drawing, with prizes ranging from a month's supply of lemonade to Bobby's very own lemonade-making class. The event had not just increased sales but had solidified the bond between Bobby's brand and his patrons. As the day wound down, the crowd thinned, leaving behind echoes of joy and the sticky remnants of a day well celebrated. Bobby, standing amidst his team, knew that the lessons from Mr.

Vozar, coupled with his own ingenuity, had brought him here. But the journey was far from over. As he helped pack up, thoughts of the future danced in his mind; new flavors, new markets, and the endless potential of 'Bobby's Lemonade'.As the last of the lemonade cups were collected and the final banners were lowered, Bobby's mind was abuzz with entrepreneurial strategies. He knew that the success of the 'Big Lemon Bash' dramatically increased local awareness of his franchise, but he also recognized that resting on his laurels was not an option. Other ambitious young entrepreneurs had seen his success and were thirsty to claim a slice of the lemonade market for themselves.

With Mr. Vozar's teachings in mind, Bobby spent the evening reviewing the feedback forms that had been filled out by attendees. The comments ranged from praise for his innovative flavor combinations to suggestions for eco-friendly packaging. Taking notes diligently, he was formulating plans to incorporate this feedback into his business model. Larger events like today's were beneficial, but consistency and adaptation would be the keys to his franchise's endurance.

Bobby decided to organize a series of focus groups with loyal customers of varying ages to understand better what kept them coming back for more. Was it the quality of the lemonade, the customer service, or perhaps the brand's community involvement? He needed to pinpoint this to ensure any future changes would enhance these elements rather than detract from them.

As he planned for the expansion, Bobby also prioritized researching his competition. He sent his trusted friends on a mission to sample other lemonade stands and report back on their findings. It wasn't just about the taste; he wanted a full breakdown - the prices, the service, the presentation. If he was going to stay ahead, he needed to know what he was up against.

Bobby didn't stop at mere espionage, though; he ramped up his marketing tactics. With the proceeds from the 'Big Lemon Bash,' he invested in social media advertising, targeted local outreach, and even sponsored small community events. Bobby knew the importance of a strong brand and community presence. He worked on training his employees to be the most friendly and efficient servers in town, boosting customer loyalty even further.

Late into the night, Bobby toiled over his business plan, and by the crack of dawn, he had a comprehensive strategy in place. He was determined to maintain the charm of 'Bobby's Lemonade' while scaling it up to meet the demands of his growing customer base. As the sun began to rise, the glow cast a light not only on Bobby's tired face but also on the bright future of his franchise. He was ready to take on whatever challenges lay ahead and was committed to keeping 'Bobby's Lemonade' the go-to refreshment in town.Bobby was under no illusions; he knew his competitors were watching, adapting, and coming up with their own strategies to usurp 'Bobby's Lemonade' as the king of citrus delights. He observed new stands cropping up, offering lemonade with exotic flavors, fancy names, and appealing discounts. It wasn't going to be a cakewalk, but Bobby was ready for the challenge.

He launched two focus groups, inviting a mix of loyal customers and potential clients from various demographics. They were presented with his new flavors and marketing materials. Bobby listened intently as they gave their candid feedback. Some comments were hard to swallow, like the suggestion to revamp his branding to something more contemporary, but Bobby recognized the value in constructive criticism and noted every word.

In line with the insights gained, Bobby decided to revamp his visual branding. He introduced a vibrant new logo and colorful cups that radiated summer energy. As for the products, beyond the classic lemonade, he crafted a line of 'Bobby's Premium Blends,' which combined traditional lemonade with unexpected flavors such as lavender and mint, responding directly to his customers' adventurous palates.

He also didn't shy away from technology. Bobby implemented an app for easy ordering and a loyalty program, which rewarded customers with a free drink after a number of purchases. The app quickly became a hit as it not only increased convenience but also generated useful data about his customers' buying habits.

Then came the 'Lemonade Days,' a weekly event at every Bobby's Lemonade stand with interactive games and prizes, which became a staple in the community. People were not just buying lemonade; they were buying an experience, and the innovation kept them coming back.

Amidst all the new implementations, Bobby never lost sight of what made 'Bobby's Lemonade' special in the first place - the fresh, quality ingredients, and the personal touch in customer service. He made sure that even with expansion, each stand retained a local feel, contributing to its unique selling proposition.

Confidently, Bobby watched as the sales figures came rolling in. His strategies were working; 'Bobby's Lemonade' held strong against the competition. The onslaught of new lemonade stands in town couldn't keep up with the level of innovation and personal connection Bobby's brand offered.

With the combination of community engagement, technology, and a keen ear to customer feedback, Bobby's little lemonade stand had grown into not just a franchise, but a part of the town's identity. And as he closed his ledger for the day, with the numbers all adding up to a very healthy profit margin, Bobby couldn't help but feel a sense of accomplishment. He had turned the sour beginnings of his lemonade journey into the sweet nectar of success. 'To the future,' he whispered, raising a glass of his signature blend to the stars that twinkled above, just as bright as the prospects of his flourishing enterprise.

~ *Fin* ~